THE LES
Of The
EMPTY CHAIR

How a Gay Medium Found Grace

BRIAN BOWLES

Through the Woods Press, LLC

Copyright

Disclaimer:

The information in this book is not a substitute for medical attention, examination, diagnosis, or treatment. None of the statements in this program are meant to replace the advice of your health care professional or medical doctor. Before doing any self-reflection program, please consult with your health care provider.

Most of the names and incidents in this book have been changed to protect the privacy of individuals and to accommodate the literary flow of the book.

Through the Woods Press, LLC

119 Western Sky Circle

Longmont, CO., 80501

CONTENTS

Introduction

THE LESSONS OF THE
EMPTY CHAIR

As the COVID-19 pandemic began to close in on our country, my hubby John said, "Brian, we better head home. This thing is going to shut everything down."

I replied, "Let's be patient and see what happens. Don't you think we'll know if it becomes serious?"

John replied, "Have you been reading the news? There's a deadly virus, and I don't want to be stuck here if a national quarantine happens."

"John, don't be such a drama queen. Remember H1N1? Just don't eat chicken and avoid making out with strangers."

There was no laughter. John replied, "I wish this wasn't serious, but everything I'm reading tells a different story. Please trust me on this. We need to get our butts home and hanging out in a resort in Florida with people from all over the planet is the last place we should be."

In a conversation that lasted less than two minutes, the trip we had planned nine months prior abruptly sent us north aiming for the top of the boot of Florida by sundown. We had driven from Colorado five days earlier, preparing for a week-long sunny retreat in the sand and sun. So, I sat there with my arms folded, watching the highway signs pass by, accepting the inner compass of my hubby. I turned up my sad music and had a pity party for one. My mom always said, 'It's fine to have a pity party, as long as you know when to leave.'

As John turned up National Public Radio to ensure I also heard the news supporting this decision, they had a short program on a museum in Montgomery, Alabama that honored the lynchings which has occurred across our country. Then, I had an idea.

I said, "You know? Dorothea grew up in Alabama. We should go see Selma and cross that bridge she always told me about. We wouldn't need to be inside or be close to any other folks, and then our journey home can at least have some purpose. What do you think?"

John turned down the radio and really considered this idea. I could tell he was really trying to make this work, because he could see how whiny I was being. He said, "Babe, let's do more than the bridge. Let's visit as many historical sites related to the civil rights movement as possible. It's not like we travel to the South very often, so let's do it. Let's read up and mask up!"

I replied, "Dorothea would certainly approve."

I grew up in a mostly African American neighborhood north of Park Hill in Denver, Colorado. Dorothea was the African American woman who welcomed me with a lemon drop and a story in her lap any time I dawned her door. Dorothea and other aunties stood watch for any child in need. These women saw through the nation's division and my privileged skin to see the child in desperate need of a welcome mat and a lesson in grace that forever changed me.

She was never paid a penny to embrace me, though mediums still proclaim, even after my first book, that she was likely my nanny or our housekeeper. Instead, she earned a PhD and worked as a professor when she wasn't caring for children who ambled onto her doorstep. The world of white eyes could never understand her presence and I will never be grateful enough to honor the way her very presence built a bridge out of hopelessness for me.

I looked in the backseat and placed my hand on Lily's head, knowing that our time with her was now measured in moments. Lily, a mostly twelve-pound beagle mixed with a dose of Jack Russell, made her a unique breed our world will likely never see again. Her large eyes and constant vigilance smelling for all things resembling food or a potential playmate had receded the last few months. Her eyes would fill with dimmed bulbs of light. Miss Lily slept as the hum of tires sailing across warm pavement made me feel like a pioneer. Her heart was being forced to operate with multiple medicines every day wrapped in a soft cheese or peanut butter. She mostly slept now, but her eyes of curiosity brightened when the sun filled the backseat. I would watch as her eyes stared at the shimmering blue ocean with novel smells, and I recognized her moments of joy taught me to see the miracle in everything.

After many meanderings that took us from Selma, Alabama to cross that notable bridge where trees cried out from across the river where Black People were hung from branches for offenses such as looking at a white woman for too long all the way to Montgomery where metallic coffins ached with the breezes of winter to honor the thousands of murderous lynchings that occurred in counties far exceeding the boundaries of what any person would define as the South, history was pleading with us to see the long shadows of oppression, but we, as a society, still only offered the shortest month of the year. Maybe, we will always debate the devastating cruelty of racism against the comforting lies White folks have used to warm the fantasies of our ancestors.

The specters of our past are haunting our present, hoping this time, we will hear the ancestors' cries in the wind as the trees quake against the songs of anguish.

We ended our four-day journey staring into the very room of the Lorraine Motel in Memphis, Tennessee, where Martin Luther King, Jr. was murdered for inspiring hope and demanding purpose belong to the dreams of every soul. Visitors of this now museum peer directly through glass walls at the very motel room where Martin Luther King, Jr. was placed on a bed after being shot on the second-floor concrete walkway by a single gunman. I stared at the queen-sized bed where he died, and I wondered, as I'm sure many of us did, what our country and the world would be if we'd had more years of his poetry, his wisdom, and most of all, his vision of unity.

Bathing myself in micro-towelettes after eating the best barbeque in the world inside a diner in Memphis, Tennessee, we both noticed the café was almost empty, and the to-go orders were lining up outside the door as many faces were covered with masks. I could now see the time had come to head home to protect ourselves from a monster only a high-powered electron microscope could identify. National Public Radio sounded like an HG Wells' melodrama, and COVID-19 was no longer the third story in a broadcast. It was the only story. The war of aliens from a microscopic world were winning, and we needed to seek shelter.

John said, "We're not done just yet. There is one more place we must visit on our way home. It is directly on the route home. This final site may seem disconnected from the journey of civil rights. However, where we are heading proves what happens when people with the greatest power pretend to be the most oppressed. With that belief system, you can justify anything."

I asked, "Where is this museum? I think we need to just head home."

John said, "The Oklahoma City Memorial. It's on our way home, and it's outside."

*

We parked almost a half mile from the Oklahoma Bombing Memorial Site.

From April 19th, 1995, this town would forever be known as the small American city where homegrown terrorists used a homemade bomb to blow up a federal building. It's not something locals are proud of, but they are sentinels of this lesson with their friendly and guarded stares, reminding you to be reverent and present. The lives of locals were impacted in far more personal ways, and many are reminded of that day by the empty chairs at their own tables.

Their eyes hope we will learn in moments what they face every day.

I looked left and saw the huge concrete figure - the large statue of Jesus weeping into his hands. This now famous monolith stood thirty feet tall as his hands directed us into the valley of Death. It was a warning of what was to come, but the statue should have been many fathoms taller to honor the tragedy that awaited us.

As you walk through the unassuming black metal gate, the chairs appeared.

Rows and rows of metallic chairs resting on glass cubes spread out in front of us.

Every chair represented a person who died that day.

Every chair, a life.

"John, can I have some time? I just can't take this in," I asked John.

He replied with a whisper, "You bet. Meet me by that large oak tree. It is called the Survivor Tree. You'll see why when you get there."

John once again researched down to the very detail of knowing the name of the tree. I'd gotten used to this after the past week of visiting historic places but knowing the name of a tree seemed a bit much, even for him. I looked around and indeed, there was one towering deciduous tree with not a leaf in sight. Winter had stripped her of her cloak, but she spread huge branches in all directions.

When visiting any memorial, such as the 9/11 memorial or Anne Frank's House in Amsterdam, I often have no clue what I'm supposed to be doing, thinking, or feeling. I had often wondered –

Why are we building memorials to tragedy?
Also, what is the right way to act?
Am I supposed to pause and read the names?

The chairs just stared back, empty and lifeless.

Am I supposed to go row by row and try to understand why two disgruntled white guys chose to use fertilizer to create a bomb to murder as many people as possible?

Am I supposed to feel?
What the hell am I supposed to get from all this?

Then, I saw the smaller chairs.

The children in the daycare on the first floor of the federal building were also murdered that day. I imagined these young babies standing to wash their hands after doing an art project or eating celery sticks with peanut butter and raisins.

I then tried to imagine the chair at the family table where a parent or a child or, more likely both, were now gone.

My inner eyes watched as imagined children kicked their legs out playfully and smiled.

How does a family continue? How does a surviving sister or brother ever play again or smile or enjoy life?

Nineteen babies going to daycare to build block towers and climb on jungle gyms died that day – that moment. Just one moment no one could ever take back.

Tears fell from my eyes, and I wanted to scream. Simple spiritual adages that had comforted me felt like cheap greeting cards only a thoughtless person would send. The anger that boiled up in me after the week of staring down the inner and outer demons of our country weren't leaving me wiser. Instead, I was struggling to get my breath and afraid to draw any attention to myself. I wish that I could write that I felt connected to the universal loss and honored the sacredness of this memorial, but that simply isn't true.

I sat on the concrete bench and looked down at my feet, counting five Mississippi's for each inhale and exhale, hoping the emotions demanding my attention coalesced into one I could hold long enough to witness. The anguish of a moment didn't yet belong to the past. Instead, these chairs caused me to consider every tragedy where the innocent had no idea their death was determined, simply by showing up to work or shopping in the wrong location or marching for a worthy cause. Panic attacks feel like God has placed her finger on the fast forward button, but your lungs and head are clawing back time to grab enough oxygen to stay conscious. The peripheral views of my vision faded, and I was staring through the old red Viewfinder my mother gave me on my birthday as the light became a circle that gripped more and more until the light was all but lost.

As I came to, a man wearing a name tag saying TERRY – SECURITY had his hand on my shoulder asking me if I was okay. I was staring at the ground and my vision was expanding again.

I replied, "Thank you, Sir. This happens sometimes. I have this weird health issue that causes me to faint at times. Please forgive me."

Terry replied, "There is no apology required, Sir. I will be standing by the column near the entrance. I'll keep an eye on you, but please raise your hand if you need my help in any way."

I never looked up. To this day, I'm not even sure what he looked like. I only know his kindness was sincere and his touch invited me back into my body. I rested my eyes and allowed the concrete to stop moving in waves before I made my way to meet John at the tree.

I approached the tree as a small group of people standing in a circle around a woman wearing a name tag saying "JULIE – DOCENT". Julie's long black hair with stripes of grey rested casually against a very long wheat-colored cable car cardigan sweater. The group was rapt with attention as she prepared to teach all of us a lesson that would certainly change anyone lucky enough to hear her words.

Julie said, "When my daughter died that day, I could not imagine a world without her in it. I likely come here and volunteer because part of me is still hoping that one day, she will find me this time. I keep hoping she will join me under this oak tree, and I will know she is truly at peace. So, what are we to learn from a tragedy like this? Why do we even memorialize such a horrific event?"

The rhetorical question hit every person standing there. Watching a mother stand and catch your eyes as she shares the day her sun fell out of the sky is a form of bravery that is hard to match. Telling the truth and allowing the questions with no easy answers hover in sacred spaces like this is no easy task.

Julia, with her long black hair and smiling face took a deep breath and found the inner voice to say, "The explosion was recorded as a 3.0 on the Richter Scale, commonly used to compare earthquakes. The explosion destroyed the federal building and damaged many other buildings irreparably. However, the four-thousand-pound bomb caused a great deal of destruction, but this oak tree survived. Can you believe this tree, directly in the path of this horrific explosion, is the very one we all stand beneath?"

Julia continued, saying "This oak tree survived. We must also survive. We must tell the story. We must never forget what happens when stories of hatred scream more loudly than love."

She lifted a gold leaf in her hand.

She raised it high above her head and ensured every person could see how beautiful it was. "When the leaves fall, we collect the leaves from this oak tree. We use electro-forming to transform them into a symbol of hope we offer to each of you today. These gold leaves are a symbol for me of a miracle that stands against the fear of that day. I have chosen to collect the miracles (and there are frankly many) from this tragic day, so the fear that allowed two men to justify murdering one hundred and sixty-eight people became a lesson for all of us to choose the hope. When we believe we are the leaf, we will forget we are the tree. Every action and inaction are choices impacting each one of us."

As I turned to leave, I almost ran into John. He'd been standing right behind me, and we both paused trying to understand how this experience impacted the other. No words filled this space. Instead, we both walked hand in hand, allowing Julia's words to push our minds through new doors that we first entered when we crossed the bridge in Selma, Alabama. Hope is a form of insanity because it disregards the current facts. However, hope builds bridges to new possibilities that cynicism and defensiveness seek to destroy.

The last light in the sky moved in rays across the distant horizon. The sun had set, and these last rays of the sun painted the bottoms of the clouds with lavender and orange.

The memorial was closing.

I stood above the field of chairs. I stared at the one hundred sixty-eight chairs, and they began to glow.

The cubes beneath every chair reflected the colors of the sunset.

Each chair celebrated a life,
a story,
a lesson,
a soul,
and the hope for every person touched by this tragedy to never forget we are not alone. No matter the story being told or the narrator offering it, stories are often the symphony of grief, inviting the chords of our own experiences to join in harmony. Stories honor the wounds of life and reminds us we have the medicine to heal.

This was the day I knew I would write this book. I wasn't certain I would share it, but I needed to remember again I was part of the tree, living in a time when we all felt separate and divided. I knew the roots of that purpose would nourish and guide me as I trusted the arc of my own stories to guide me back to my own wholeness.

I can only offer you my story.
That is all I am and all I ever will be.
You, as the reader, will decide if these stories are reflections of you. However, I can only offer my stories, because they stand as a testament to the power of hope in the face of doubt, loss, trauma, and heartbreak. They stand as a reminder that the hardest moments become the greatest lessons.

There is a Grace that has always found me in the hardest of times in life, and I will never pretend to have any of her rivers or tributaries mapped against the lessons of my soul. However, I can say, for certain, she is real and reliable and true to the compass of any heart on any path.

I trust my stories to remind you of yours.
That has always been the language Grace speaks into my life.
So, I offer you my stories, so you can know your own.

Chapter 1

WHAT HAPPENS WHEN VOMIT TRAVELS AT THE SPEED OF LIGHT?

Picture me, a thirteen-year-old kid in Denver, Colorado, one summer evening in July. My hair had more mousse than required, and my hairstyle was complete with a rat tail. I had a skateboard with an anarchy sign painted on it. I could never ride it, so I just carried it in my arms and walked around, looking angry. The album "Beauty and the Beat" by the Go-Gos played on my bright yellow Sport Walkman CD player with matching headphones. I was a nerdy as hell bad ass with a sixteen-sided D&D die in my pocket just in case a dungen master needed some hit points to defeat a monster.

I was never that sexy guy standing by the red sports car at the end of Sixteen Candles. I have always been more of a Duckie kind of guy, if you know what I mean. If you don't, please know how deeply sorry I am that you did not grow up in the eighties: big hair, shoulder pads, bands with names like the Go-Gos, Bananarama and Depeche Mode. It was a level of cool this world will never know again.

"Come on, Brian. We've ridden the Wild Chipmunk five times!" June yelled, trying to make herself heard above the loud hum of rollercoaster chains rattling against old wood structures. Crescendos of screaming voices drowned her out as the coaster dropped down the first (and only) exciting hill.

I loved the Wild Chipmunk ride, because the small metal coaster had separate cars and was strangely frightening—it made ninety degree turns, the nose of each blue car careened off the edge of the track, but then it always ripped back, and you were saved at the last second. I was in the Alvin cart leading the pack, and Roberta and June managed to double up in the Simon cart behind me. As the small individual carts made the first turn to slowly ascend the first hill, I was in rollercoaster heaven. I could hear June's laughs as Roberta downloaded all the best gossip with each crank of the chain getting us to the peak of this adventure. Roberta said, "Jimmy is seriously noshing all over Vera, who is certifiably nuts. She had big tits in fourth grade. Why does my chest look like Kansas?" The "-as" of Kansas got loud as the individual car dropped down a medium-sized hill, and I was certain onlookers were trying to figure out why "Ass!" was the word she chose to scream out on a rollercoaster.

The Wild Chipmunk was not a child's coaster. Although, I must admit, the soundtrack of Alvin the Chipmunk's high-pitched voice demanding that we "Have a Merry Christmas" on a hot July night made no sense. This is why both June and Roberta stared at me with bored eyes whenever I looked back to see if they were having as much fun as I was. "Christmas in July!" Roberta yelled, dripping in sarcasm. "Gag me with a spoon."

Do you see what I mean? The Eighties!!!

Later, I followed June and Roberta towards a large, spinning disk with rainbow-colored lights spreading out from it in all directions. Little did I know that I was being guided towards a moment that would change everything.

There was a long line and as we got closer, I could smell the new car smell. The song "I'd Like to Teach the World to Sing" was playing over and over again. The title of the ride was displayed in technicolor, dreamy lights that enchanted every moth west of the Mississippi: THE GRAVITRON – RIDE OF THE FUTURE. We all looked at each other. Roberta said, "That ride looks so lame." So, with quiet agreement, we all stood in line, looking irritated and as disinterested as possible. But our constant tapping of our feet and our hands twitching at our sides revealed a building excitement.

#

Roberta had long, curly brown hair, tussled in circles. When she got nervous, she chewed her hair. (Was it her conditioner that smelled like watermelon-flavored bubble gum? Likely!) My other friend, June, was the quiet one. While Roberta and I fought for the millisecond of space between each piece of the conversation, June just smiled and kept quiet. Her long blonde hair and stunning cerulean blue eyes made it impossible for her to diminish her natural beauty—even with her frumpy red sweatshirt. She always wore her hair pulled back tightly with a turquoise scrunchy. Her eyes wandered here and there, but June was never fully present.

June and I were very close. I knew the echoes of anger and alcoholism that bounced along the hallway to the hollow-core door that separated her room from that world of chaos. Few words about her father's abuse were ever spoken, but the markings on her arms from the spiraled metal coil in her college rule notebooks gave her away. She dug into her arm with the coil, tearing tributaries of flesh away as she tried to obliterate memories and reclaim her innocence. But below each layer of June's icy resolve, she was trying to dig through memories to find the escape hatch.

Sometimes, we hurt ourselves because that way, we can control the pain. We can predict the hurt. The fresh cuts made zigzags resembling the symbol for water on petroglyphs against June's flesh and sometimes, the blood seeping from the deepest wounds pooled against her shirt. The older marks left a scar, and I would caress my fingers in gentle swirls over her cuts as Joy Division's "Love Will Tear Us Apart" played on a mix tape I gave her. I hoped my songs traveling from teenage angst to Bach's Mass in B Minor would compete with the world of anger and hopelessness that scratched at her reality every day, but I knew they wouldn't help her escape.

"Should we get premium tonight?" June asked as we waited in her room for Roberta's brother (whom I secretly called 'Sexy Antonio') to drop her off. When we'd first decided to huff gasoline, we'd joked that we'd "purchased premium." Our first time, we'd bought three gallons at the Sinclair station near Holly and Yale Boulevard, but our little metal gas can was for one gallon. The clerk never offered us a refund, and we'd pulled away sheepishly...we knew we were breaking some big law. We were criminal masterminds.

Tonight, we had some leftover gas in her garage. So, we huffed it directly from the silver can and poured some into the rolled-up purple My Little Pony t-shirt she handed to me. Every time we inhaled; the world softened. The pounding sound began in my ears. June heard the same sound—our warning to stop. As we huffed gasoline and ether, and any other intensely chemical concoction we could get our hands on, the harsh worlds we both inhabited began to quiet. June said, "Brian, drench the shirt and let's take it with us so we can fly during one of the rides." I drenched the shirt and rolled it into a circular motion like an egg roll and folded it neatly into the plastic grocery bag she handed me. Then, I rolled it up tightly and June placed it in the small bead purse she carried everywhere (which mainly held her lip-gloss, gel pens, and eye liner).

#

As we crisscrossed the final steps into the Gravitron, June reached into her purse and we both took a deep breath through a small hole in her purse. Roberta pretended not to notice as she began rolling her hair more intensely and shoving more strands into her mouth. The people directly behind us made grunting sounds and looked confused. They were irritated that the line was moving so slowly. The single deep gasp of toxic gas fumes didn't have the full effect, but the world began to soften with a ringing sound I had come to know well. We didn't hear the words the line boss spoke, but Roberta interrupted my flight, saying, "Get going, guys! Come on! We should get on this time."

As we crossed the red velvet cord, our leering line mates behind us made a quick departure, punctuated by curse words, making it obvious that we were the final riders for the night. So, I felt even luckier to have this chance to ride the Gravitron. The circular ride looked like a record player, with multiple flashing neon lights, and blinking lights running together in streams.

The ride attendant, a tall, red-headed fellow with freckles on each cheek, looked like an evil version of Ronald McDonald. His afro, forehead acne, and silver braces made him look like he was part of the ride somehow. "Pick your spot!" he yelled as he held the control box in his hands as he ushered us through the four-foot-wide entranceway into a dark, enclosed room. It looked like a TV remote, and I kept looking for the large brake that rose out of the floor near every rollercoaster, but there was only a box with a few colorful buttons and a black cord.

The walls of the Gravitron were large, red velour rectangles, each one had a chain dangling from it. Each rider had to choose their spot against the wall, then latch the chain across their body. It was a simple latch and an inconsequential chain—it made the ride even more exciting, because this chain was not exactly screaming "Safety is our biggest concern."

We found our spots and buckled in. I fished the My Little Pony t-shirt out of the deep front pocket of my Bermuda shorts and June and I both inhaled the lingering fumes. Roberta was three spaces down from me. She looked over at us, then rolled her eyes and looked away as if she had no clue why we were sniffing a child's t-shirt.

A soft hum filled my ears, the lights dimmed, and the voice of the evil Ronald look-alike floated through the static of the intercom. "You kids ready to experience zero gravity?"

Roberta, ensuring her public-school education was put to good use, said, "Not zero gravity, idiot! It's called centripetal force."

The operator smirked as he leaned in through the gate. He bellowed into his microphone: "I can't hear you!" The bright lights of the carnival sparkled behind him and caught his reflective metal braces. They gleamed—he looked possessed.

"Are you ready, little wooses?," the operator's voice boomed.

The room erupted with screams of glee and anticipation. We watched through the four-foot opening as the operator touched the buttons on the floating black box. The dark, circular room began to rotate. The neon lights around the perimeter of the walls began to flash. The music droned on and on ... "I'd like to teach the world to sing...."

The revolving hell ride went around so fast, we stuck to the walls. It all occurred so quickly, This turntable wasted no time. Suddenly, the redhead's voice boomed through the ether, "Are you ready to die? The floor is about to disappear, kiddies."

The floor dropped away, everyone screamed. We stuck against the red velour padding, unable to move, and the Gravitron kept spinning and spinning.

"You're my last ride tonight! Enjoy a bit longer in zero gravity!"

Roberta yelled, "Not zero gravity!"

"I'd like to teach the world to sing...." The room spun, the lights flashed, screams of glee and joy soon turned to hopeless wails. Faces paled, despondency set in.

"You're not a bunch of little sissies, are you? Raise your hands above your head if you're a faggot! Then, the faggots can get off and go cry to their mommies. Anyone a faggot? If one fag raises their hand, the ride will come to a stop. Raise your hand, faggot! You're making everyone else suffer."

In that moment, I knew I couldn't raise my hands. It couldn't be me. I looked around. No one raised their hands, even though the ride had whirled past excitement into despair and fear.

No one wanted to be the "faggot." So, we all accepted our fate and hoped the nightmare would end.

The heavy air and dizzying lights made the world go slower as the ride seemed to go faster. I saw one person's face transposed onto another. I tried to hold the vision, but it faded as quickly as my eyes could adjust. Then, many faces became a swirl of color. I was freaking out. My feet were dangling off the edge of an abyss. My breath quickened, as my mind fought to find ground. The spinning continued, and I kept thinking to myself, we are doomed. I pushed against the force of motion, but the hands in the dark reached forward to restrain my purpose.

Then, I surrendered.

Though my body was in chaos, stuck against the red wall of Hell, I was at peace.

I was floating in a void, a celestial harbor, a haven.

Stars appeared around me.

I could see endless solar systems and beautiful streams of light travel across my eyes.

I was observing the world from the edges of a distant galaxy.

Then, I was no longer spinning. I was suspended in light and watching my body and my dear friends struggle as every square inch of their bodies were forced against the red pads, even causing them to turn their heads sideways, giving into the force of this moment.

I was completely at peace.

In my thirteen years on the planet, I had never felt disconnected from my body but connected to every living thing. The faces moving in a mirage revealed bodies of light holding steady against the waves.

Suddenly, my stomach lurched sideways—like a car with a flooded gas line or a faulty starter. The screams seemed to increase with every rise of fear. I was back in my body, and the acid in my stomach was building. A nausea started to take shape and build in intensity. I tried to force it down by swallowing, but this force was also out of my control. The curved muscle of my diaphragm contracted. My head snapped forward off the red-cushioned rotating wall. Everything in my thirteen-year-old stomach - pepperoni pizza, a root beer float, and two funnel cakes - emerged all at once. Jackson Pollack would have been inspired. The vomit flew away from my body and immediately flew right back on a person two to three cages over.

My fellow passengers started retching too. It was a catharsis that everyone joined, because, it turns out, making this ride four times longer, impacts every living being the same way. The vomit flew in every direction, and the retching sounds became louder than the screams.

The screams finally stopped.

Silence filled the whirling room.

We heard the red-eyed demon say: "Oh my God! Disgusting!"

He applied the metal brake ... a screeching sound ... the ride slowed ... and slowed ... and slowed ... and finally ... it stopped.

All the lights went out, and the song on repeat disappeared.

A few people dropped their heads and vomited on their shoes. I noticed the floor had returned beneath our feet.

I looked around. The main doors we entered had been opened, so a stream of light filtered in. The bright lights from the outside world filled the dark space, but no one moved. We all waited, silent, as the circling world of blurred faces came into focus. Multi-colored vomit had been splattered across every rider, head to toe. Every one of us was stuck hopelessly in place, held against the wall by a flimsy chain. Our bodies had stopped rotating, but our brains were still swirling.

When we undid our chains, some of us couldn't stand up and fell. Some gripped a neighbor to remain standing. But whether standing or lying on the ground, we were all still spinning through space, trying to find the ground.

No one could get to those doors that invited us back into the world we knew before this moment.

Then, someone said, "That was awesome! Can we do that again?" We all started laughing. No one was spared—all we could do was laugh.

Even looking back now, it made perfect sense—evil Ronald's diabolical plan had backfired completely. The Gravitron looked like the set of a laundry detergent commercial and we were all the BEFORE pictures. I confess, seeing that red-headed, curly-haired operator (covered in puke), cursing up a storm, trying unsuccessfully to clean himself off with one napkin was both deeply disgusting and sincerely satisfying.

I will never forget the moment good 'ole Roberta said: "Well, if you think about it, at that speed, it is likely that we all vomited on ourselves."

I could only think: Does this make it less gross or more gross? At this point, degrees of comparison fail.

I regained my balance somewhat and tried to stand. As I did, I felt the strangest thing...the person next to me was gripping my left hand. I looked over to see my friend June smiling at me wryly, as if we had just endured another amazing adventure together. Her puppy-dog eyes were bright blue, and I strained to see if her smile was the enameled one, she used to survive or the real one.

This was a smile of pure joy. In this moment, she was herself. This reality reflected her inner life far more than the one we normally inhabited.

We both left that ride changed forever. I knew there was a force far greater than I had imagined. I knew that we were not alone. I knew the stars in the sky were a reminder of who we truly are. I had a million more questions, but I knew we were more than our bodies.

That changed everything. I hope others won't need to be trapped in a circular ride from hell hearing a Coca Cola song on repeat with vomit flying everywhere to discover this truth.

"Did you raise your hand?," June asked.

"No. I didn't see anyone raise their hands," I replied.

"I raised mine," June said, as the groups of kids started to exit the palace of vomit.

I turned back and whispered, as if keeping her secret, "Why did you raise yours? You're not gay."

June then smirked and said, "No, I'm not, but my best friend is. He's just not ready to say it yet."

I turned back and followed the line into the night sky. I had no words at the time, and I pretended she hadn't said it. However, it was three months later that I finally found the words to tell June.

There are few examples of love I have found greater than the night June grabbed my hand with her right and held up her left hand knowing that one day, I would find the courage to do it for myself.

Chapter 2

THE DAY THE COLOR
PINK DIED

"Are you Mary Ann's son?" her gentle voice asked from the other side of a phone that spanned over a thousand miles of phone lines and satellites. She had been given the sacred purpose of angels to share the ending of a mother's travels.

"Yes, I am," I said. Before the words were spoken, the force of what was to come had already reached my heart. Now, it was just the words, the human words required to match what my heart already knew. This moment feels so spacious but in empirical terms, it was less than seconds.

"I'm sorry you were left on hold for so long. I'm Madeline, your mother's nurse since she was moved into our hospice program. We met a few months ago. When you called, your mother was actively dying. I held her hand. Your dad had only left her side thirty minutes ago. I'm sorry to tell you, but your mother has died."

My mother's bedroom often felt like an altar where so many stories were carried to God's ear through the smoke rings released from her chain-smoking lungs. In her eyes, I practiced saying the parts of me that I was scared would shock the world.

I don't remember the details of what followed hearing my mother had died. The world was still moving, and clocks were still clicking against the gravity of the sun, but I was now in the tides of the moon. Only a small part of my brain was managing the niceties required to complete a phone call like this. I did tell them I would prefer to be the one to let my dad know.

I wanted his memory to be the voice of his son telling him his wife of over fifty years had died. My father had dutifully held vigil by her bedside in a nursing home for many years, but the moment when Death places a period on a person's life still leaves me breathless.

"Dad, I have something hard to tell you. Mom died soon after you left her side this evening at the nursing home. Madeline, her nurse, just let me know."

I will never forget the gasp and the one-word response that flowed from his rational structured mind when he said,

"What?" That word spoke a million prayers to a million gods in one moment.

He was now floating out of orbit, and I was a planet in a different galaxy. I'm the difficult child in this family of four. I'm the rebel to everything my family declares as sacred. I now understand that role was waiting for me before I even arrived.

My mother had died, and my father's companion for over fifty years completed her last breath. Our worlds would never be the same, but our gravities were challenging even Galileo.

I flew to Colorado, where memories of riding in my dad's used Cadillac and eight tracks playing Gordon Lightfoot, the Eagles, and strangely the Star Wars soundtrack always felt like home. The final leaf had fallen from her trunk, and Winter began after many moments in a nursing home in Colorado Springs where my mother faded from this world slowly. We would tell the world she had dementia, but the truth was harder to honor.

The receptionist at Mount Olivet Cemetery, a Catholic cemetery in the metro Denver area, guided us to a small office with three-ringed binders stacked perfectly as we waited in awkward silence for the mortician to arrive. The three-ringed binders had pages upon pages of coffins resembling an old Sears catalogue where coffins in every color invited me to wonder how many families picked the steely purple coffin that looked like a Batmobile or the flesh-colored capsule that looked way too much like a sex toy. I wondered if the people working here were preparing dead folks for prom or porn. Someone had clearly become confused at central office.

"Did you do the obituary?" my dad said.

"Here it is, Dad" I said as I raised the laptop screen. The file named OBITUARY_MOM glowed as I clicked it open. My dad pulled the screen close to him and looked down through the bottom of his bifocals with an earnest gaze.

"Brian, I told you to keep it simple. Just the basics. Did you do that?" my dad asked.

"Yes, Dad. Just the facts. What's the problem?" I replied, hoping to bring some levity.

As he re-read the two paragraphs that just stated the facts and followed the typical structure where you state the obvious, I saw him staring at the one sentence I knew would cause him concern. I had hoped he wouldn't notice, but no such luck.

After you describe the deceased, obituaries typically explain who the surviving loved ones are and their children and their grandchildren. It's basically a family tree sentence. I saw it blinking at me on the computer screen and I knew this was a statement I could never undo, change, or alter.

HER YOUNGEST SON, BRIAN, MARRIED TO JOHN B., HAS NO GRANDCHILDREN BUT A LOT OF GRAND PUPS.

I had been married to John for over twenty years at that moment, and my mom had grown to really love John. She'd often say, "I'm still not okay with you being gay, but I'm grateful you're with John. Does that make any sense?"

In that moment, I knew this was exactly what my mom would have wanted, but obituaries and funerals are not for the dead. These statements for the local papers must align with the lines we draw around family and what is acceptable and what is unacceptable.

My dad finally said, "It's fine. Just please remove John. You do know where I live. Colorado Springs is not exactly a liberal community. Would you then submit these to the Denver and Colorado Springs papers?"

I replied, "Dad, you asked me to write the obituary. You never mentioned for me to not include my family in it."

He said, "Brian, John is a part of your life, but I'm asking that you not include this. People in my community will not understand, and you know it will upset your brother. Can't we just have this be about honoring your mother?"

My brother's name and his wife and two children who I had never really known held space in my mother's obituary like flags on claimed land where I never had a chance. My brother insisted my then boyfriend John not attend his wedding, and I politely said, "I am not able to honor your beloved by dishonoring mine." That was twenty-five years ago, and the cracks in our family's foundation had never been repaired.

There was no battle or argument to be had in that moment. We each had roles and we each knew the right lines to say in the scene. We'd repeated this one so many times, but my mother's passing would not move the tides of hurt that defined the dance between a father and his gay son. I would never be the son my father wanted, but I knew I needed to be the son my father needed.

So, in this world, at that moment, I simply said, "Okay."

I updated the obituary, and I removed not just my husband's name. I also removed mine.

I could not exclude my partner in life, because it felt untrue. Death invites an honesty and an awareness, but clearly, this would not be that moment. I looked at the words on the page that would be held in digital worlds for many years to come marking the death of my mother, and my name being excluded perfectly encapsulated how I had felt since I was a child – the problem child.

Then, the funeral at my dad's very Catholic Church, the one true holy church for all eternity, occurred. I decided to not have John attend because I knew I couldn't protect him through this memory. I was too vulnerable, and I knew my focus needed to be on caring for my father. That was where my mom would ask me to place my heart through this moment.

As I stood next to my father in the front pew, my brother stood on the opposite side of my dad. His wife and two children stood next to him. My father was the sentry for the resentments and pain we had all defined ourselves by over the years. My mother's weirdly metallic pink coffin, perfectly crafted for a drag queen, was in front of us. I clearly was too distracted by the obituary drama to track how Rainbow Bright's coffin ended up being selected for my mother. I know she liked pink, but I was left wondering which discount rack offered this hideous chamber that even a drag queen would reject.

After the part where the priest talked about my mom and how much she loved to help with Sunday school, the priest said, "Mary Ann has been suffering for many years now. God is proud of her journey and how she suffered to know his grace."

Why is it we allow the people least competent to speak to the memory of a person's impact in our lives in those rituals of loss? He clearly didn't know the resilience and strength of one of the wisest people I'd ever known. Also, his version of God was scary as hell.

At the end, because my dad is a highly respected deacon in the Catholic community, fifteen deacons were there to assist in her celebration of life. So, as they wheeled her coffin into the sun outside the church, the priest and the local bishop took a golden wand and dipped it into a golden bucket of water and blessed her coffin. Every deacon and priest needed to follow suit and they couldn't be outdone by the previous. So, each elevated soul resplendent in golden robes stepped up to the plate and dipped the golden wand into the water to bless her coffin. It looked like she died in a horrifying accident at a water amusement park somehow involving a Pepto Bismol truck. I'm sure your imagination can do the rest.

I kept thinking to myself, why didn't they bury her in her swimsuit?

The next day, there was the burial, and I dreaded the moment of watching her coffin descend into the ground and being surrounded by the very people I am least comfortable with being any level of vulnerable. At the funeral, some of my dearest friends knew I needed them, and I never even had to ask. They were there and holding space for the awkward silences, but I remember my dad saying, "The burial is private. It's just for family."

I immediately approached the awaiting hole in the ground. I saw her pink coffin from hell that was, in no way, improved upon by the light of day. The color pink died that day as I stood by my father on the exact same side the previous day. My brother with his family took their spot on my father's left side. The grey cast of clouds with the sun barely breaking through matched perfectly the world my mother inhabited for many years before her death.

Then, a miracle occurred.

I heard a door shut on a van, and I looked back to see my husband's father and mother stepping out of their vehicle. However, it wasn't just them. John's entire family was there. They all approached, and I reached for them as they covered me in proper Scandinavian midwestern hugs with two feet distance and no bending at the waist. I wanted to crawl into their arms and scream from the highest mountain how much I loved them in that moment. Instead, I composed myself again and returned to my dad's side.

We had never been together in any way until the moment of my mother's burial. It will likely never occur again. However, on that day of grey skies and pink coffins, I knew she had made that moment possible.

Chapter 3

CAN A LEATHER DADDY CHANGE A LIFE WITH A KISS?

Every Good Friday, when I was young, my Catholic mother would insist we be in our bedrooms from noon to 3 PM to honor the sacrifice of Jesus Christ our Lord and Savior. It was to remember the stations of the cross and honor the path Jesus took to his crucifixion and acknowledge how he gave his life for our sins. Even now, at the very ripe age of fifty, I'm a bit confused by this. Was his sacrifice for our sins? Did he prop the door open to Heaven when he died?

I'm a bad bad bad bad Catholic (Yes, every single bad was required). I would sit there for five minutes and stare at the sacred heart of Jesus picture and see him crucified on the cross. It all seemed both violent and confusing.

My mom would say in her most earnest voice, "Jesus died for you so you could live. Judas betrayed him with a kiss. We don't want to be Judas." Huh?

My little gay-boy-self kept thinking, "Did he die for me?"

When a priest who you believe is Jesus's buddy tells you that you are carrying the demon of homosexuality and that these very desires are from the heart of a demon, that kind of makes you look at that Jesus fella and avoid him at parties. The silver cross hanging from a person's neck was like garlic for my inner vampire trying to find a different sun where the version of me created in God's hands could grow too. Over time, as I came out repeatedly, some friends stayed, and others left. It seemed hanging out with that Jesus fella was not good for keeping friends so I broke up with him.

I was tacky about it. If we had cell phones then, I would likely have broken up with Jesus by text. If Jesus saw me as broken or possessed by some fabulous demon, then the relationship simply wasn't going to work in the long run anyway.

The child in me that prayed to him for my mother to find peace and my dad to choose me had long become a whisper even the trees couldn't hear.

#

The time of AIDS was a time when Death was the uninvited guest at every party. That period of time is impossible to capture in words, but the experience of seeing gaunt faces and the hopelessness to offer a lifeline as the tides of disease stole away their light one moment at a time was our shared experience as a community for many years. I was in Washington DC in 1990 starting college and beginning my adult journey as a gay person.

My roommate Jimmy was a stocky black-haired teddy bear Italian fella from Jersey who became my big brother as we watched I Love Lucy episodes every morning before I headed to my college campus for classes.

I had landed at our home on 609 A St. SE by moving in with a boyfriend. The relationship was Britney Spears' level of toxic, but Jimmy was the eyes of grace that found me every day to remember things get better. I had been forced out of the dorms on the Catholic University of America (Yes, it's a real university) campus due to being gay and, after many months of couch-surfing, this shared home became my saving grace.

Jimmy's best friend was Shaun, an adorable blonde-haired porn star with only joy in his heart. When Shaun's HIV status became AIDS because his t-cell hit 132, Jimmy decided to do a goodbye gathering as Shaun prepared to die at home in South Carolina. We all dressed up and showed up. Shaun was held, loved, and celebrated by every person in attendance.

Jimmy was in tears that night as the night came to an end, saying to me, "Brian, we will never see Shaun again. He is likely to die in the next few weeks, so I meant it. You need to volunteer with me at the Whitman Walker food pantry. I do it every Tuesday and Thursday night, and you need to join me. You cannot forget you live in a world where sex can kill you and not protecting yourself is not an option."

I held him in my arms as we both wept. This giant teddy bear of a man had saved my life so many times by feeding me and clothing me I could only offer the obvious response to this moment.

"Yes, of course, I will, Jimmy."

Two weeks later, Jimmy said, "Okay. I've got you set for your training next Saturday, but, in the meantime, can you do something important for me this week. My friend Chuck's husband just died two weeks ago. There's an ACT-UP event in Bethesda, Maryland, and it's on the red line past the Brookland exit. You'll need to be there by 1:30 P.M. which, if I have it right, means you will exit your college campus at noon to get a meal and arrive on time."

Jimmy handed me the flyer and I replied, "Don't worry. I've got this."

He said, "Brian, Chuck is a great guy but he's a little rough around the edges if you know what I mean."

"Jimmy, I'm cool. I'm nineteen years old now. I've got this." Jimmy handed me a ten dollar bill for my fare and lunch.

As I got off the DC Metro Red Line in Bethesda, I pulled out the flyer with two hot fellas kissing. The flyer read: SILENCE EQUALS DEATH. I didn't frankly get the idea of this at the time, but I was afraid to ask and look stupid.

I found the location in the atrium of an NIH building by following a group of gay men from the Metro. I didn't even need to refer to the map Jimmy gave me. As I entered, I saw a bunch of men kissing. It was a shocking site as people in white lab coats walked by in a hurry. Seeing two guys kiss in public was still uncomfortable for me, but I would be lying if I didn't acknowledge that this approach was clearly effective and impossible to ignore.

Jordan, a tall man with salt and pepper hair, was carrying a clipboard and a red marker, came over to me and grabbed my arm.

Jordan said, as he guided me across the makeshift kissing rectangle, said, "You must be the preppy guy partnering with Chuck today."

As Chuck's name came out of Jordan's mouth, I was standing across from Chuck, an older leather daddy with a goatee with grey patches in dark hair. He was wearing a t-shirt with a leather vest and jeans. He was a stocky man with blue eyes that stared right through me.

Yes, my loins were burning. I don't even know what the hell loins are, but they were definitely burning.

"Howdy! I'm Brian. Jimmy asked me to be here today. He's sorry he can't be here," I said.

"Chuck here. Jordan, can I get someone a little less.... preppy?," Chuck asked as if I wasn't there.

Jordan looked at me, and I could see the gears working. Jordan said, "I can fix him up a bit. Let's start with removing this rugby shirt. You have a t-shirt on underneath this?"

I nodded my head as my rugby shirt was taken off and Jordan nodded as if to let me know my white t-shirt untucked with jeans made me look passable.

Jordan said, "Will this do, Chuck?"

I smiled back at Chuck and begged him with my eyes to accept me as his partner.

Jordan then said, "Will he pass for today? You don't have to have sex with him."

They laughed, as Jordan departed. Chuck sighed and looked my way as Jordan walked off with his clipboard being waved to motion for more guys to follow him. That's when I saw for the first time what assless chaps were. It looked like two bald heads had lost their owner.

I was regretting my decision more and more as I felt completely unprepared for this. I was left standing across from a leather daddy that had already let me know I was definitely not his type.

Chuck then said, "Okay Brian. Come closer. I won't bite…yet."

He held me close to him, and he whispered, "I'm sorry, Brian. You're with a leather community Act-Up event so I want to ensure people know you're part of us. I didn't mean to embarrass you. You look pretty hot in your jeans and t-shirt, so you'll thank me later."

I replied by saying nothing. I just surrendered to his grip on my body, and I eventually rested my head on his shoulder as he moved gently from side to side. I could feel his warm breath on my neck, and I was seriously burning in my loins now.

I looked around as I rested on his shoulder moving to a sound only Chuck could hear and watched men around me kissing. They were smiling and kissing. It was beautiful. I didn't know the first thing about this group, but I knew they were fighting for better access to medical care for our brothers with HIV and AIDS.

Then, Chuck said, "Okay Brian, are you going to kiss me or not?"

Chuck pushed me back and I was a little taller than this broad-shouldered daddy with the blue eyes of an angel. So, I leaned forward and placed my lips on his. I then froze. I know it's insane, but I started to make an inventory of everything I'd eaten in the last twenty-four hours and wished I'd brought a thousand starlight mints for this moment. I was royally screwing this up. I then felt his tongue gently pushing against mine seeking entry into the foul-smelling demon's lair where a garlic bagel and a bowl of chili I'd found for lunch were being digested slowly. I refused to open my mouth. Instead, I just moved my lips against his like a puffer fish on the side of a aquarium.

Chuck pushed me back again, and he said, "You're a terrible kisser. You seem like a sweet fella. Can I help you? You'll never get laid in DC if you can't entice someone with your tongue. How young are you?"

To avoid answering that question, I just blurted out, "Yes! Yes! Please help me," as if I was bleeding on the side of a dirt road and he was the only person in sight.

Chuck then smiled and began to laugh seemingly to himself. He then said, "Okay. Pretend you find me attractive." Check!

He continued, saying, "Are you worried about your breath?"

I nodded. It's hard to explain, but he asked this question in such a disarming way I wanted to cry.

"Brian, it's okay. I like a man's mouth. I like tasting a man's tongue. I can't stand toothpaste mouth. So, can you trust me?" Check!

"Brian, it starts with position. You're a little taller, so place your head sideways as you come in for the kiss. Let me respond by choosing the angle you offer me. Just don't come at me head on, because that's how grandmas kiss. Got me?" Check!

Loins still burning!

"Well, come in for the kiss already, and I'll guide you." Check!

As I came in for the kiss, I turned slightly sideways. I could feel my lips press on his and I immediately froze once again.

He pulled me in for a hug and wrapped his arms around me. Chuck said, "You know, Brian. Kissing is about trust. Every man is here kissing in front of the world of health officials hoping that we can trust them. Do you know how important this kiss is? You want to show the world of federal officials our love matters. Our love is serious. Our love is… forever." His voice began to quake as the word forever escaped his lips. I felt a strong exhale on my neck, and I could feel his emotions pushing tides of sadness and heartache across our bodies. I gripped him back and placed my right arm on his upper back to hold him better.

Chuck then said, "That's nice, Brian. Do you see what you did there? You responded to me. You reacted to me and became stronger as I began to…" Then, we just stood there in one another's arms as the world disappeared. I heard some shouting chants and others kissing, but we were in a world of our own.

I then whispered, "Can we try again?"

Chuck then said, "If you can't say it with some confidence, absolutely not."

I replied, as I felt my back straighten, "I want to kiss you."

Chuck then said, "Are you a top or bottom? You don't even know yet. You're a baby gay. I promise you this. No man will ever let you make love to him if you don't know how to kiss him. If you can't access my mouth, I'm never offering you my body. Shall I take the lead this time?" Check!

I said, "Yes", and I felt my trepidation as the word came out.

Chuck then said, "I want to kiss you. Will you give me permission to take the lead? I need a stronger Yes, because I don't want to push you into spaces you're not ready to travel." Check!

I replied, holding him tighter, "Yes."

He pushed me back from him, and we stared at one another for a moment. His blue eyes closed as he moved in for the kiss. His slightly arched neck and grip on my back pulled me into him. I can't offer a single detail. I can only say that when his tongue penetrated past my lips, a dance of connection occurred I never knew possible. I was so afraid of my sexuality that the idea of enjoying it hadn't crossed my mind.

Chuck placed one of his hands on the lower part of my back and the other on my neck as he kissed me in ways that left me transformed. Then, suddenly, he stopped and pulled me close to him. Chuck held me and I returned the grip of my arms against his back matching his intensity. I didn't notice he was crying. I was so overwhelmed by the connection, and he rocked us sideways as the gentle sounds of him crying washed over me once again.

I didn't know I was that bad of a kisser. Then, Jordan appeared. He placed his hand on Chuck's back and said, "Chuck, it's okay. It's barely been three weeks since Reggie's passing. I knew it was likely too much. I'm happy to step in for you."

Chuck said, "No, I'll get my shit together. Brian is a perfect partner for me. By the way, he's got potential to be someone's great lover." They both laughed but I could see Jordan's tears. Clearly, Jordan loved Reggie too. I didn't know anything about their story, and I was afraid to ask. As Jordan walked away, Chuck held me and rocked side to side.

Chuck then said in my ear, "You're a sweet fella. You know that?"

"I feel the same way, Chuck." Chuck then wiped his snot and tears on my shoulder. I know it sounds crazy, but it was a beautiful moment. I just held him and began rocking him too.

"Can I kiss you again, Brian, my little preppy friend?" Chuck said in my ear. He didn't even wait for a response and began to kiss me once again. This time, I kissed him back. I was voracious and felt the strength in my core and spine tighten against his tremulous grip. I pulled him closer to me and placed my hand on the back of his head, kissing him deeply. He then tightened his spine and pushed against my force matching it and dipping me back as he kissed me deeply.

Chuck then pulled me close and placed his head back on my shoulder rocking us back and forth once again. Chuck then said, "I wish you could have met Reggie. It was many years together, and I still can't believe he's gone. It's strange. It doesn't feel real. Do you know what I mean?"

Yes, I do. Yes, I certainly do.

I replied by holding him closer to me and Chuck continued, saying, "If he can see me right now, he's laughing his ass off. Have you had anyone close to you die of AIDS?"

"Yes," I replied as Shaun's face flashed before my eyes. He was still alive but actively dying at his sister's home in South Carolina.

"Will you promise me something, Brian? Promise to protect yourself? This is a terrible disease. Promise me?" Chuck said as we rocked back and forth. I replied by kissing him once again, and I felt my spine stiffen as I dipped him sideways. He quickly grabbed my arms and gently placed them behind my back as he kissed me deeply.

Then, he whispered in my ear, "I need to hear you say it, Brian. Do you promise?"

He then pushed me back and we stared at one another.

I replied, "Yes, I will. I promise." I wouldn't keep that promise perfectly. The edges of sexual adventures in my youth pushed me to crazy places at times, but I would be reminded of that moment many times. I would see his face many times, pleading to be safe in this unsafe world.

Chuck said, "Thank you, Brian. You just might be a leather guy. Have you ever tried on a leather vest or a harness? That's likely too much to throw at your preppy face this early in your journey, but you are have the energy of a leather guy. One more kiss before we go?" Hell yes!

So, as we moved side to side, the world of that atrium in the National Institutes for Health and the men around us began to bring me back to the world of the here and now.

Then, it was over. The two hours had passed, and Jordan brought me back my shirt. I held the shirt in my hands and stared at Chuck. I was certain he would carry me out in his arms and we would ride into the sunset together, allowing our bodies to be our compass.

Instead, he smiled and said, "Great meeting you, Brian. You need to work on kissing well and don't go fishing for my tonsils. The mouth is an arena, and you only go down to the center of my Earth. There's so much area you missed. Didn't you notice how my tongue covered every spot in your mouth? Enjoy the connection but don't go fishing!"

"Thanks Chuck for... being here with me. I'm sorry about Reggie." As I stared at Chuck, I could see a taller man with black hair and a mustache smiling at me. His big eyes looked at me with a kindness and a gratitude I imagined I made up in that moment. It wasn't until many years later that I realized Reggie was indeed present.

His eyes filled with tears again, and he said, "Brian, you have your whole life waiting for you. We will stop dying at some point. So, you need to live. Be safe but enjoy being in love with a man. It's a powerful thing to love a man. Don't let this disease take away…"

"Chuck, I know… I understand what you mean."

Chuck's beautiful eyes filled with tears made him look like a child I desperately wanted to hold and tell him things would be okay, but I knew that would be a lie. Chuck said, "Brian, love someone. Hold them tightly, even as the world tries to tear you apart. It's all worth it. Trust me. I need you to promise."

"Chuck, I promise."

Chuck held his arms on my shoulders and gripped them tightly.

Jordan waved to him, and the event was clearly ending. People were peeling off, and the atrium was slowly being reclaimed by the men and women in white lab coats.

He then said, "You'll hopefully find a good preppy lover. Although, unfortunately for the twinks, you're likely a leather guy. You need good training from a proper Daddy. Just not me. Look me up in a year if I'm still here and I'll give you more lessons."

I walked away feeling as if every nerve ending had been ignited. I was in desperate need of a cold shower as I placed my backpack over my shoulder feeling the weight of my Biology final remind me of the work ahead.

I never became a leather guy. I've always continued to be the nerdy fella desperate to find the nearest D and D club. However, I moved to Nebraska at the end of that year to finish my undergrad in the world of corn fields at another Catholic school. My parents didn't realize there were hot gay farmers, but the moment with Chuck was one I would never forget. Seeing Chuck continue life after Reggie's death was inspiring and a reminder that the ones left behind are searching for their beloved in the eyes of every person.

Jimmy's voice boomed on the phone, "Brian! We miss you in DC, but I'm proud of you for doing so well in school this year."

"Thanks Jimmy! I'm coming to see you this fall. I wish I could join you guys at Hotlanta this spring."

Jimmy laughed and said, "Brian, you're a prude. You would freak out at Hotlanta. Let's keep it real."

I replied, "Too true. You know me well."

Jimmy's bass voice became more tremulous, and I could feel his thoughts trying to coalesce the words together to take flight. He said, "Brian... I attended Chuck's memorial service today. He still talked to me about the preppy guy who can't kiss every time I saw him. You really showed up for Chuck that day. I can't thank you enough."

The weight of his words landed on my heart, and I felt as if I couldn't breathe. I forced some words to the surface of this ocean of grief, saying, "Oh Jimmy. I'm sorry. Chuck was a good man. I..."

Jimmy then interrupted me, saying, "Brian, Chuck is still a good man. He's no longer on a human map, but his spirit is everywhere now. We'll see our brothers again someday. I'm certain of it."

I asked Jimmy, "How do you know?"

Jimmy said words I will never forget on the phone that day. He said, "Brian, I know. The many brothers we lost to AIDS are now the wind on a fall day, the sun in the winter sky, and the blooms on the cherry trees. They are everywhere. One day, you will know this."

I borrowed his certainty, because the weight of grief was confusing and mostly just left me angry as hell with the consequences of life and love. I was twenty-one for only three months. I didn't know Death was a friend yet.

Almost every consequential man I met on that journey of coming-out in Washington DC died well before the time of most.

Jimmy eventually died of a broken heart less than ten years later, and only the gang would understand just how real that is. The world moved on as the new cocktail of drugs appeared, but so many of the men who showed me how to be the best human I could be died during that season of AIDS.

Jimmy was one of the only ones left from that family of men, and his death ended a chapter of my life in so many ways.

I now see how these many brothers in spirit are guides and sentinels for my journey as a medium. I needed to know those beautiful men were never really gone. Instead, they had transformed.

Chapter 4

THREE KNOCKS, TWO SCOTTS, AND ONE PRAYER

The First Scott

When I teach mediumship courses, I often do an activity where I place my walking cane on the floor, and I have us all stand in a row on one side of the cane. I then tell them the simple instruction, "If you have a YES to any question, you are asked to step across the cane. The YES or NO questions often refer to experiences. One example is, 'Have you ever been told you are not welcome at a church simply for who you love?' Participants will choose which side of the cane makes the most sense for them. Then, I'll ask participants to look to the left and the right to see your friends here that hold that same experience and therefore, that same wisdom.

I'd then say, "If you did not cross the cane to the side of YES, you then see your peers who did as your teachers in this area. If you want to know more, reach out and ask them if they would allow you to interview or ask them questions to better understand."

We'd start with less vulnerable topics such as, "I am a child of divorced parents. Cross the cane if this is true for you." Then, we'd process what they learned as a child of divorce and how it informs mediumship.

One peer said, "Well, for me, when a medium says my father is here, I don't always know which father they mean. So, I am waiting for the medium to discern between my two fathers so I can trust who is with us. Does that make sense?" We'd all nod in affirmation.

After the connections started deepening through this exercise, we'd explore racism, homophobia, and sexism to acknowledge arenas where we experience privilege or oppression. This often leads to dialogues about honoring every person's view and being careful to avoid assumptions that become biases and even prejudices in the work.

After the students really understand the process, I then end with the same question each time. I say, "Okay guys, this one is a vulnerable one. Please only cross the cane if you feel safe to do so, and please know you have a choice of whether to disclose this. "I have been at risk of suicide in my life. Cross the cane if that is true for you."

I will never forget the time when the entire class of twelve students all crossed the cane. I then stepped out of my facilitator role, and I crossed the cane, saying, "This means every one of us has a wisdom about suicide. Your journey with suicide will serve you powerfully in the work of mediumship."

I had come to know that every experience where I carried shame seemed to be a powerful aspect I could then offer to the work of mediumship. It was as if a chord existed in my instrument a Spirit could play, because we found a common resonance in our story. It feels like a harmony.

In that moment, after the workshop, I began to reflect on how my life traveled from the dark room of hopelessness to this moment. I realized, in that moment, the journey of mediumship was also a curriculum for my healing and my journey towards wholeness.

This lesson of suicide all began in the darkest parts of my mind and the light that found me was in the eyes of a person who knew the medicine of a witness. He offered me his eyes instead of his advice. He gave me his presence instead of his judgment. I would come to recognize in writing this book that he was one of the most important teachers I had in my mediumship journey.

It all started with me saying to myself repeatedly -

I want to die.

Now, I'm living in Omaha, Nebraska, a solidly red state in the US meaning deeply conservative and voting Republican in every election. I had just exited Washington DC to escape that toxic relationship and to get my degree completed.

Omaha was a tough place to be, handsome farmer Bob notwithstanding. Strangely though, it was where I confronted being gay. I was up against the most despicable, biased homophobe in the world—ME.

Suicide came to visit—*again*. We had hung out from time to time since I was a young fella.

There I sat, in my lonely apartment. I was getting ready to fill the bath and I had a date with a razor and my wrist. I was miserable, disillusioned, disheartened. Here marked three years of feeling isolated, depressed, and scared of life. I had planned that night for almost a month. The doors of all the choices and strategies I had slammed shut, and I transformed a fate of hopelessness and powerlessness to a choice that gave me authority and agency. I had turned on the sad music and lit the candles. I folded the note of goodbyes and gratitudes imagining the moment those who loved me would discover my soliloquy.

Then, I entered the bathroom and turned off the water for the ritual to begin.

Suddenly, there was a knock at the door.

I froze like a child being caught halfway out the window when a parent catches you sneaking out. I had no plans of someone coming by that night, so I waited expecting the wrong knock on the wrong door to move along.

Then, I heard the second knock, and this one was even louder.

"Damn it," I said to myself. "Can't I even kill myself?"

I waited again, but I realized this was not a mistaken guest. Someone was there for me.

The third knock broke the haze of my perfect plan. I blew out the candles and wrapped myself in a towel as I approached the door. Scott O'Hanlon stood there peering through the window with his sharp eyes and lion main of brown auburn hair parted nicely in the middle. After a couple months of downright darkness, a new friend, Scott, was now standing at my door.

Saying he was a friend is generous. I'd met him at the local gay bar, and we had a kind of sort of crush on one another.

"Brian, what the hell is going on here? Candles, depressing music, and a bathtub filled with Morrisey and cheap bubble bath? This can't be good. You're either getting ready to have sex with a depressed British fella or you're a complete wreck. Is there a hot British fella on his way over?"

I shook my head from side to side.

"So, I came over to get you naked, but it appears I picked a bad time. Are you stressed out?"

I replied, "Not really. There's just lots to do this week, so tonight isn't my best night."

As he stepped into the living room from the kitchen, he saw the note. I'm the weirdo that put SUICIDE NOTE on the folded-up notebook paper. Scott held it in his hands, and I watched him move it from side to side trying to figure out what to say.

Then, he peered directly at me, and he asked, "Are you planning on suicide while listening to crappy eighties music?"

I nodded. I stared and kept nodding. I knew there was no lie big enough to escape this moment.

Scott then said, "You still get to decide, Brian. Would you rather take a drive with me or end your life? I won't beg you, but there is always another way."

I nodded. It is still amazing to me how a simple nod changed the course of my life. Some force greater than my little frightened mind made a choice for me to live. I nodded and my future was uncertain again.

Scott took me out of there immediately, drove us to a lake in the country, and chatted with me for nearly six hours. He listened. He laughed when I laughed, cried when I cried. When he asked about suicide, he was comfortable with the word in his mouth.

He finally asked directly, "Be honest with me. Brian, was it going to happen tonight?"

"Yes," I said. I was returning to my body with every word that haunted me on the inside losing its power as I spoke to them on the outside.

Scott asked the most important question, saying, "What are your reasons for wanting to die?"

I spoke to them one by one as he listened with a rapt curiosity. He never interrupted; demanding Life speak more loudly than Death.

Instead, Death had the stage, and he became an audience member, asking only for more and more information. As the words formed in my mouth, they lost their power.

As I heard myself say the reasons, the narrator looked confused and uncertain where the story would travel. He laughed at the hardest scenes by joining them. He helped me to see the lonely story needed more characters.

Scott then said, "Brian, I remember the day I decided to end my life. I walked out to my truck, and I sat in my truck. I put on my seatbelt, and I laughed at how insane it was to buckle up for safety. I then checked my rearview mirror. The garage door was closed, and then I turned on my truck. I didn't have any idea how long it would take to work, but I put on my favorite album."

I asked, "Do you mean Pet Shop Boys?"

Scott looked forward at the small lake where we parked and gently said, "Sting. It had to be Sting. Soul Cages filled my truck, and I waited to die."

"What happened, Scott?"

"That's the craziest part. The garage door was not insulated, and the carbon monoxide couldn't build up. So, I eventually turned off the truck when the album ended and I said out loud, "Alright God! If it's not my time, at least help this not hurt so bad. My life, in many ways, began that day. That was one week before I got sober."

I said, "Scott, I can't believe that story. You seem like you have your shit together. It's...."

He interrupted, saying, "Brian, we are all so good at pretending to be okay when we aren't. We become experts at this, don't we?" I nodded. "I have no idea why I didn't die that night. I frankly thought to myself I can't even kill myself correctly. Then, over time, I started to trust something, or someone wasn't going to let me depart that night. You know what I mean?"

Yup!!!!!

"Scott, how is that any different than you knocking on my door tonight? Three knocks."

He looked straight ahead, and I felt like we were going to make out as every good eighties' movie tells you. However, he just looked ahead and eventually, I joined him. We both stared at the lake knowing the words of this moment were complete.

As he started up his truck engine, he said, "Brian, I had no plan to go out on Tuesday. I just knew I needed to go to the bar that night even though I'm in sobriety. It had been over two years, but something made me go to the bar, and that's when we met. This moment we are having is filled with coincidences or, as Mama Jackman will say, answered prayers. How about you and I get some rest and we head to Mama Jackman's place this afternoon?"

"Who's Mama Jackman?"

He replied, "He's an old queen who seems to have a particular set of skills to help the broken feel whole again. He's basically Yoda with ugly sweater vests and too much cologne."

I replied, "I'll be ready."

As his truck pulled up to my apartment building, he said, "Brian, can I trust you to be alone for the next six hours?"

"Scott, I'm not alone anymore." I didn't believe in the whole God nonsense yet, but I knew the man who knocked on my door three times did nothing less than save my life.

The Second Scott

Mediumship, for me, started with the realization that I needed to figure out this whole God thing or Higher Power (sounds like a failed eighties song) or Creator or Insert Fancy Spiritual Term Here.

I remember well staring at the bizarre images of a man bleeding on a cross with gold plates and chalices gleaming on a table, where we were asked to honor that we weren't worthy before going up for Communion, the actual body and blood of Christ. It was all confusing and I never could understand why the men wore the dresses and also why they chose flats instead of heels. It was a half-assed drag show, but the stakes were your soul.

All humor aside, I remember when I first told the priest in confession that I thought I was gay. He told me I was possessed by the demon of homosexuality and that I needed to pray for an intercession by God immediately to save my mortal soul.

He was half right.

I went home and I prayed for likely the first time in a way that felt real.

I tried to pray the gay away.

It didn't work. I don't know what I thought prayer would be like. I guess I thought a magical de-gayifying dragon (Gayifying is not a word yet, but we can make it work!) would emerge from the celestial plane and relieve me of my gayness in a magical swarm of smoke and butterflies. The fact I thought that should have been a clue phone I wasn't yet willing to answer.

Yup.

How I ever imagined this prayer could undo me is hilarious now, but that little boy wanting that priest and community to love and accept him meant every word.

I prayed again and again, "God, please please please release me from this curse. My parents deserve better. My mom works all the time, and my dad is a Catholic deacon. How much more holy can you get? Pretty please with sugar on top!" (Again, there is lots of evidence that this gay thing was maybe sticking around.)

I'd wake up every morning and I noticed immediately my magical prayer had failed. As funny as this seems now (because it is), that little boy felt cursed and abandoned by God. I began the journey of apologizing for being alive and taking up space. I began to feel that my way of being the best version of myself was to hate myself.

Somehow, that weirdly felt like being loyal to God. I would do a better job of hating myself than God ever could. I would destroy myself long before the slings and arrows from the demons residing in the ninth circle of Dante's Inferno could rise-up to abolish me. I would also never ask to be worthy enough to belong to the same house of faith where my parents found God. Instead, I would politely slink away and hope that my parents would see I was protecting them from the darkness where the light of God couldn't touch.

Then, I met an angel, a real one but with a bald head and multiple sweater vests perfectly dry-cleaned and a crippling amount of Drakkar Noir (the cologne men wore in the eighties that likely made women gay). He introduced me to a different God, and I would never be the same. I would not be alive if this one had not crossed my path when he did. This may not be a parting of the Red Sea kind of miracle, but it broke a path wide across an ocean of self-hatred where I returned to me. The one and true Holy Roman Church may not qualify this as a miracle, but, to me, these acts of grace are answered prayers to the hurts that can drown us. This was another soul reaching to another soul. This was Love in a form that is undeniable and powerful and shattered the world of self-hatred and self-pity where I had established residency.

As I nervously counted my fingers, feeling the nubs of broken flesh where fingernails should be, I knew I was ready to do my third step in Omaha, Nebraska where I was completing my bachelor's degree.

Scott Jackman (AKA Mama Bear Jackman) stared at me from the couch while I sat cross-legged on the floor having one of the very first sincere chats about God. His bald head flanked by sandy brown hair with silver streaks near his ears made it clear he was old enough to be my father. His eyes had built a trust with me over time I had never imagined possible. Scott was my sponsor, as he was to many other gay men in Omaha, Nebraska during the year of 1992. Our Friday night meeting became a church where the songs and stories the most courageous people I'd ever met sang to parts of me that were either asleep or left for dead by me in memories too heavy to hold. My songs of sexual abuse, being homeless after coming out about being gay in college, and finally leaving an abusive and crazy relationship were the songs playing on my radio station.

However, in those meetings, I found a harmony to my stories and every person's eyes held their own story that weirdly related to my own.

Although it became clear over time that I wasn't an alcoholic, Scott said, "You may not be a drinker, but you're just as crazy as all of us. Replace 'thinking' for 'drinking' in the AA assessment, and you'll see that you belong to us. You're likely an Alanon, which doesn't make you less crazy. It frankly might make you more because you're addicted to your pain."

He was my Gandalf with shiny brown loafers and tassels and a bald head that reflected light across the seas of my despair. He was barely five feet tall, and no one would mistake him for a wizard, but he was the unlikely Moses for my dramatic as hell desert. You can justify almost anything when you have decided the weight of your burden is greater than everyone else. You can lie, cheat, and steal from any soul unlucky enough to cross your path. I had become the monster that priest imagined in that confessional booth.

After attending the meetings and hearing the harmony to my sorrow, I was beginning to believe this path might even work for someone like me. Instead of feeling separate from the world around me, I started to see myself in the eyes of every sister and brother around those tables. For the first time in my life, I started to understand pity was not love.

I will never forget when Ruthie Ann, sober for fifteen years, told her story. She told her dramatic journey with alcohol where she ended up offering hand jobs in her van outside liquor stores; she woke up one morning with actual icicles in her hair. She laughed and we all joined her. She then said something that opened that God door just a tiny bit.

She said, "When my sponsor told me to pray, I told her to go away. She turned on her heel and looked me dead in the eye saying, 'If you only have time to pray while giving a guy a hand-job, maybe use both hands and pray at the same time. Can't you multi-task?'"

I knew then she was my people. If you could invite me into your hell and leave me laughing on my way up the stairs, then you were a friend of mine. She then talked about how easy steps one and two are:

Step 1: We admitted we were powerless over alcohol – that our lives had become unmanageable.

Let's see. A twenty-one-year-old wanting to end his life in a bathtub is likely the definition of unmanageable. Check.

Next! This was going great so far.

Step 2: Came to believe that a Power greater than ourselves could restore us to sanity.

I loved this step because you don't do anything. It was like deciding to clean your house. You don't have to clean the damn thing, but hell, you've decided to, one day, clean your house.

Yup! I was loving the twelve steps. I frankly felt kind of gifted at it.

Then, that evil step three appeared out of nowhere. I'd heard the queens sing those steps every Friday night for months, and I even droned on and on with them just like I did at church when I was kid.

My sponsor Scott called me on a Monday afternoon and didn't even ask how my day was going. Rude!

"Brian, I gave you the five questions I want you to explore, which means you need to do some writing on them. Step 3 is critical. I think it is the difference between someone who gets their sanity and others who further their insanity. I want you to share with me how you pray. I also want to know about your idea of God. You can't say Dolly Parton is your God again. It's cute and funny, but it won't save your life."

Scott Number Two was much older and less pretty to look at than Scott the First. Scott the Second was so bossy and put so much pressure on me. I wasn't even a drinker. I was just a whiner. Maybe, this whole step nonsense needed to be abandoned in favor of another dramatic relationship with a crazy sociopath I somehow knew I could fix.

It was that Sunday afternoon when we attended an AA conference and Ruthie Ann was speaking. She said almost word for word how I'd felt about the first two steps. She had the same issues as I did with the third step.

Ruthie Ann continued, saying, "Prayer is when you know you can't walk another step, so you fall to your knees and ask whoever is listening to please tell you how to stand again. Rinse and repeat."

"I will never be able to tell you how much my life changed when I gave up the fight and allowed a different God to walk in my door. It wasn't about the alcohol at that point. It was when I knew I wanted to be here. I wanted to live."

I wanted so badly to know what that would feel like. I had spent so much time pretending I wanted to be here but the whole 'fake it till you make it' idea was getting old. I had come to believe that the blowtorch that went around and around my gut would eventually destroy me.

Five days later, Scott gave me a sheet of paper during the Friday night meeting. As the folded note arrived after being passed along the gayest circle of men in the Midwestern United States of America, his eyes bore into me. That nightmare watched until I unfolded the letter and began to read it.

The note said,

THIRD STEP
MY PLACE
SUNDAY AT 1 P.M.
LESS WHINING, MORE WRITING

Somehow, when God entered the room, I wanted out. I was not willing to join another group of Moonies who walked around starry-eyed saying, 'God loves me more than you!' with their silly faces of devotion and self-righteousness.

Yack!!!

The man with the white-collar people called father used the word "god" in his mouth but he was the face in my nightmares. His touch dimmed the light of the sun and made my body a stranger.

However, this Scott fella had not misled me yet. He had become a trusted confidante in short measure with his soft timbre baritone voice and his gentle nods to let me know he heard every word of my tempest. If there was a God, he was likely the perfect messenger.

So, I decided to let the word 'God' return to me, but I knew she would need to be wearing heels. The old white guy with sensible sandals had let me down too many times with his gavel that this church would need to play Madonna songs and raise arms of love to drag queens and offer carabiners to my lesbian sisters to climb any wall the world demanded of them. This God had to be special and personal and love the freaks.

Would that God show up on Sunday at 1 P.M.? I doubted it, but I hoped She would.

As I pulled up the Golden Girls house where Scott was living temporarily until he landed in his own place, I paused and placed my hand on my heart. I knew I needed help, and that night in the bathtub was not far enough in the rearview mirror to trust myself. Bernie, who we all called Bernice, greeted me with his Bostonian accent and hugged me. He gave me a plate of cinnamon rolls and a large orange juice. The other two queens of the Lost House for Homos sat in their robes while watching football. They waved and I began the descent into the basement where Scott lived.

Scott sat on the couch looking over my written assignments and waved me over. He then leaned forward and looked right at me, saying, "Are you ready for the Third Step?"

A long pause ensued as words to this question seemed ominous and confusing. I didn't want to fake it this time. This needed to be real, or I was out of there. I asked, "How do you do a third step? I don't know if I'm ready."

He replied, "Love, you begin to pray and believe someone is listening. It's that easy, Brian. That's your third step. It's a start of a conversation. It's a chat with God."

I laughed and looked right at him, saying, "No one's listening, Scott. Let me make this perfectly fucking clear. I've asked for help my entire life, and I can assure you no one is listening."

Scott looked right at me and looked like he was about to stand, saying, "Really? Have you ever prayed?"

I confidently announced, "I've said thousands of Our Fathers and Hail Mary's. I was brought up Catholic. God wasn't listening. Not once."

Scott leaned back and took a drink from his glass. He then said, "Brian, you've acknowledged your life sucks and you can't continue to operate based on your own will, because clearly, it's not working all that great."

I replied, defeated, "Yup." I had no idea "Yup" was my prayer. It was how I acknowledged how powerless I was.

"Let's try something different this time." Scott grabbed two card table chairs sitting against the wall and set them up right in front of me. The bronze metallic chairs stood opposite from one another.

Scott continued, "Brian, this chair is you. When you sit in this chair, you are your thoughts, your feelings, and your emotions. I should call this the crazy ass chair but that's being too kind. The other chair across from you is the chair of God. Let's start with you telling me about your ideal God."

I could feel (and didn't like) where this nightmare exercise was likely heading. I decided to play along for a little more time, because I had come to appreciate the group of women and men at the meeting on Friday nights. Besides, one fella was hot, and I knew that connection could lead to some great distraction. That was likely my God for all those years – distraction.

How could a God exist when monsters with collars touch into the light and leave behind the dark? That old loop of anger and hurt primed up again but Scott interrupted my train by saying, "Brian, tell me about the God of your understanding. If you prefer, we can say Higher Power."

I replied, "Higher power? That sounds like a CEO of a fitness company. Let's work with this whole God thing. For me, God has always been this old white guy with long flowing hair, just like Fabio. He also wears very sensible sandals, and he wasn't very nice to his son when he was bullied here on Earth. He also has a weird obsession with his angels being children and having no clothes, kinda scary if you asked me."

Scott laughed again, and he said, "I agree with you. That's not my god. So, I get it. You don't want that weird old white guy with sensible sandals. Who is your God that you could trust?"

I replied, "Scott, I really don't know. I don't. Can you tell me? Why can't I have your God?"

"Brian, never ever let another person tell you about God. That is the most personal and sacred relationship we have in life. This is yours and I would never push my version of God onto you."

I replied, "Okay, Scott. I give up. This is starting to feel like a puzzle I can't solve. What do you need me to do so I can say I'm done with Step 3?"

"Brian let's do something different than you've ever done. Let's ask God together. If you could place your hand on your heart for me and then consider this question: Who is someone you know, without a doubt, loves you exactly as you are? Who could you count on as a kid?"

Her face appeared immediately.

I didn't even have a chance to think it through. I gave a second longer for Snuffalupagus to show up, but all I could see was Dorothea. Dorothea, the elderly African American woman who lived near us when I was a child, always greeted me with kindness and a smile. She gave me lemon drops and read books to me. I remembered falling asleep in her arms wrapped up in a blanket as she rocked me. We were one of the only white families living in a mostly Black community, and she always took me in when I knocked on her door.

Scott continued, saying, "Brian, use that person to make sense of this whole God thing. Imagine she is the one in that chair across from you and she is here to answer any question you carry on your heart." He paused for a while, and then he said, "You're ready. Take the BRIAN seat first."

I sat down, and I felt the chill of the metal against my back. I looked across and saw that empty chair. Scott artfully stood at my side, but he was just out of my peripheral vision. His hand gently touched my shoulder as he said, "Okay, Brian. You have Dorothy sitting across from you."

I corrected him, saying, "Scott, her name was Dorothea. Think Door-O-Thea. Does that make sense?"

He said, "Yes, Love. Sorry about that. Has Door-o-thea passed?"

I replied, "Yes."

Scott had this tender way of making sentences I had heard sound new. He said, "Oh Brian. I'm so sorry for your loss. I'm sure she will have a lot to offer us today."

I knew he meant it. I had heard that expression so many times, but those words rose like starlings on a lake in the sincerity of his presence.

Scott continued, saying, "Okay Love, what do you want to ask Dorothea? If she is your God, what would you like to ask?"

I froze. The space between me and the chair across from me felt more distant than ever. I even felt nauseous as the room began to tremble with me.

"Brian, it's okay. Let's take this slow and easy. Every conversation starts with just a few simple words. As you look at that chair, allow her to fill in the space. Allow yourself to remember her face, her eyes, and her smile."

I did. I could see her gentle eyes, her curly hair that often looked askew. I knew she wore a wig, because I'd never forget the time she greeted me with her bald hair and a white nylon cap. Her glasses rested against her chest with the silver edges and the matching silver chain. She looked back with a kindness and compassion I had longed to see for so many years.

"Close your eyes and let her image fill your eyes. Brian, when you're ready, say whatever is on your heart."

Then, I was moved even further into the fantasy of this moment. The living room with the brown cloth couch and the wooden rocking chair with a wicker seat that was ripped began to enter the space.

I then said, "Dorothea, are your proud of me? I know I've let you down and I am sorry for being such an asshole. Sorry about that. I'm just so sorry for being such a mess all the time." This was basically a repeat of everything I had ever said at the twenty meetings I'd attended.

Scott tapped my back and said, "Great job, Brian. Can you ask her a question?"

I then asked, "Okay. Dorothea, are you mad at me?"

Scott then said, "Okay Brian. Let's have you switch your chair and sit in the GOD chair. Let's see what Dorothea has to say."

I stood up and sat in the chair directly across from me. The metal wasn't cold. The chair felt bigger somehow. That gave me the chills and I could feel me rebuilding my walls when Scott said, "Okay Dorothea, Brian is wanting to know if you are mad at him. He feels he has let everyone down in life. He feels no one loves him. What would you like to say to him?"

I opened my mouth, and nothing came. I felt my legs tensing and the arc of the metal chair dug into my scapula as I stretched my legs writhing away from this moment any way I could.

Scott placed his hand on my shoulder, and I softened into his warmth. It felt as if his touch was filling me with the sibylline liquid of the moon. I winced to hold back the tears.

Scott then said, "Dorothea, place your hand on your heart. Brian wants to know if you are mad at him. Are you mad at him?"

I placed my hand across my heart, and I felt myself leaning forward. I then opened my mouth as this voice emerged from a place unknown, saying, "Oh Brian. You are my chosen son. I love you and there is nothing you can do to ever escape my love."

Scott gently nudged me to return to my chair. As I sat in that chair, the tears started to fill my face, but I wasn't allowing myself to cry. I had become an expert at pushing away any feelings and this would not defeat me. I would be the one fella he'd fucked with this way that would not fall into a pile of my own mucus.

Scott said, "Brian, did you hear what Dorothea said?"

I replied, "Yup." He was starting to make me angry, so I was rebuilding my walls. This had gone far enough.

Scott then said, "Brian, what question do you have about placing your will into her hands, recognizing your life is out of control and unmanageable?"

I looked right at him, hearing the metallic chair groan as I shifted backwards, "I don't have any more questions. This exercise is crap."

Scott placed his hand on my shoulder and kept his eyes towards the floor. He then said, "Place your hand on your heart and ask her just one more question. Remember the third step is really about prayer. Don't you have a question about…"

"I got it, Scott. This is so stupid. Let's just get through this." I then placed my hand on my heart, and I immediately saw her staring at me in a new way from the chair across. I thought for a second it was her and this was a big practical joke, but then I realized it was the her that lived in my imagination. I decided to play along.

I then asked, "How do we pray? To make others get off my back and do this whole God thing, can you tell me how to pray?"

I leaned forward and felt myself stand and immediately sat in the chair across from me. The warmth immediately embraced me, and I weirdly smelled the faint smell of cigarettes her husband smoked and the lima beans cooking on the stove.

Scott said, "Place your hand on your heart. Brian wants to know about prayer. Do you have any guidance for him?"

I placed my hand on my heart, but something was different.

I started to rock in the chair, and a voice emerged from deep within, saying,

"Brian, prayer is a love letter that never ends. Sometimes, you write one to me and other times, I offer one to you. Every time you pray, it is meant to remind you that the pain is always temporary, but the love is eternal. I am always by your side."

Scott then asked, "How can Brian know you're real? How can he know his prayers are heard? He is such an optimist about the world but a cynic about himself."

I once again felt my body move forward in the metal chair, and these words flowed from another river in another place, saying, "We are never alone, my dear one. We are never alone. Who do you think sent the man to your door to knock three times?" Then, the tears flowed and all of the sudden, Scott's arms held me as I shook with a fury of emotion I never knew lived inside me. The anger, the fear, the sorrow, and the loneliness erupted in waves and earthquakes as a voice from the other side opened a door in me I would never close again.

Scott looked at me now on his knees in front of me holding my hands with so much love, saying, "Brian, are you ready to choose life? I sure hope so because I've grown to really love you. We all have. You're home. Will you promise to choose life?"

I felt the weight of this question and I wish I could say my words rose to my lips quickly. I wanted to mean it, and after a short pause, I replied, "Yes. I do, Scott. I promise."

I have never been in the river of suicide again.

That storm quieted and if that's not an answered prayer, I don't know what is.

This was the beginning of a new life with more mistakes, more lessons, more failures, more successes, and equal amounts of grace that would never be measured.

Dorothea led to many other mystical connections and the right teacher has found my eyes when I have needed them most. The spirit world seems to offer the right anchor to hold me in the hardest of tides. Prayer today feels like breathing. It is a constant conversation with the grace that always guides me back home.

#

"Scott, I'm sorry, but Scott Jackman died." I had just gotten the call from our dear friend Vince. Scott the Second died on a business trip in Regina, Saskatchewan from the pneumonia that greets you at the door of Death when you have AIDS, a disease none of us knew he had.

Scott and I wept together on the phone as the sudden passing of our dear friend and mentor became more and more real with every passing moment.

It would be roughly five years later when another call from Vince arrived, and this time, it was Scott the First. The famous DJ had played his last song and died suddenly in his sleep.

It was impossible to imagine being in a world without these two friends.

After six months passed and the memorial service I attended in Omaha, Nebraska with the other men impacted by the lives of these two Scotts, I remember sitting in the living room and asking for a sign. My prayer was, "Can you send me a sign that you're here with me? I can't do this life without you."

I heard Mama Jackman's voice say, "Instead of a sign, how about I offer you a chair?"

Chapter 5

GALLOPING GERTIE AND RESONANCE

"We have an exciting video to watch today that explores some fascinating aspects of wavelengths and sound," Sister Benita said as she rolled the metallic cart with the TV and VHS tape player attached with a black strap.

Yawn alert. I sat in my wooden desk, doodling profound wisdom in my notebook, ready to fall asleep (again) during a video in my Junior science class at Regis High School. The window shades dropped as Sister Bonita continued her explanation of the stunning video we were about to see. NOT! The videos in Sister Bonita's class were mostly 70's videos explaining the reproductive system or dissecting the philosophical tenets of sedimentary rocks.

I was in my acne phase. The potholes on my face bled and oozed even as I applied multiple layers of salicylic acid solution. I was an awkward sixteen-year-old gay boy at an all-boys Catholic high school. Our grade in PE was determined solely by whether we wore a jockstrap or not every day. Yes, the PE teacher checked. For every two negative marks you receive in the gradebook for not wearing a jockstrap, your grade goes down a full letter grade.

"As you observe this video, I want all of you taking notes. This will be on your test," Sister Bonita said as she pressed PLAY on largest and heaviest VHS tape player in the world sitting on a metal cart next to a large box TV that weighed more than me. She killed the lights and the room went dark.

I lowered my head. In the dim light of the flickering video, I reflected on the tragedies of my adolescence.

During the credits, Sister Bonita wrote on the blackboard the names of students who were talking or were guilty of other infractions. Sketchy black and white images appeared on the screen.. The Tacoma Narrows Bridge title finally appeared through the VHS tape fog.

From my second-row seat, I was amazed. The bridge began to dance. This was a real-life episode...a bridge designed to allow people to cross a small section of Puget Sound in Washington state was moving up and down as if a demon had possessed it.

The announcer's deep bass voice with equal parts curiosity and horror said, "On a particularly windy day, the newly finished bridge began to shake and move until it eventually collapsed. But why? Why would the Tacoma Narrows Bridge collapse during strong winds?"

At this point, I guess I'm checking to see if you listened on the day this infamous VHS tape filled the screen of your own classroom so many years ago.

Okay, smarty pants! Why?

All right. I guess I'll tell you. Must I do everything? You can't cheat off me during the pop quiz.

Resonance

That's the fancy technical term. When the wind increased on that fateful day, the wavelength of sound in the wind matched the wavelength in the suspension cables. Resonance occurred. It was as if the wind was literally playing the strings of the suspension cables as an instrument. It was as if Black Sabbath came to town and tore up an electric guitar, except the bridge wires were the strings of the guitar, perfectly tuned to respond to the pitch of the mighty wind. The resonance was so intense that after the waves of movement went up and down the flimsy wooden beams, the bridge collapsed.

How does the destruction of the Tacoma Narrows Bridge fit into my story? Well...resonance.

I'm amazed at how that video explains the foundation of mediumship. The tuned chords of the wind matched the chords of the cables, and they *resonated*. In that classroom in high school, watching that black and white video, I was being introduced to a part of me that would not come to surface for many years to come.

When working as a grief counseling intern at The Denver Hospice for my master's degree in counseling with an emphasis in marriage and family therapy (that's a mouthful!), I was asked to attend an afternoon meeting where a famous local medium would be speaking. My reaction sounded a little bit like this: "Woo hoo! I can't wait to hear a nut job speak about talking with the dead. It is very disrespectful for people like this to prey on others' sorrows."

Yup.

That about summarizes it. However, one of my teammates encouraged me to attend as a way of respecting other people's points of view. I obliged, and I tried to get a better attitude in the process.

As I walked into the room late, the leaders of the hospice and other staff members all sat in rows as a middle-aged, brown-haired woman (with stunning highlights), a bright red dress emphasizing all her curves, and high heels for days stood confidently in front of us and discussed her work as a medium. Her name was Deb, and she was seriously stunning.

Her smile and self-effacing humor could have disarmed North Korea. She was a superheroine, apparently, but I was not impressed. I was certain she was manipulating people and deceiving them somehow. I imagined she'd done advance research and had secret access to the hospice database. This, I decided, was the only explanation.

Deb came up to me after her talk and said, "You're a medium too. You may not believe me, but you are called to this work. Come to my office and let's chat. Maybe you should schedule a reading."

Woo hoo! The crazy woman in high heels just told me that I too can speak to the dead. You might think that I would have been grateful or curious, but instead, honestly, I was even more certain of her deceit. I was disgusted and confused. Why would a person like this be allowed to come into a professional setting?

I went back to my office in the bereavement section of the hospice and told a colleague, Lisa, what Deb had said to me. "I think it is so disgusting," I said, "that they would encourage this type of deceit. I am not going to waste my time having someone manipulate me for money."

My teammate left my office quickly, clearly shaken by my words. I followed her; she was in tears.

"I'm so sorry if I offended you. I didn't really...."

"Brian, Deb helped me out more than anyone else when my son died. She...."

"I'm sorry, Lisa. I didn't mean to upset you. I didn't know."

"Brian, you're being so dense. I'm not sad for me. I'm sad for you. Your closed mind will keep you from experiencing something miraculous."

"I didn't mean to disrespect you. It's just that...."

"Brian, if you really want to show that you respect me, go see Deb. If Deb told me what she told you, I would make an appointment to see her as quickly as possible."

Resonance. Sometimes, I hate resonance. Okay. Not really, but this was that moment. This conversation would cause me to pick up the phone and make that call, feeling confused and embarrassed. It was guilt that made me pick up that phone.

I can't imagine my life if I hadn't made that call.

After booking a time with Deb's husband, her scheduler, I arrived at her home early and read through a basket of cards in which people had expressed profound gratitude for her support. In card after card, people stated that Deb had given them hope for the first time after a serious loss. The pictures in the cards showed mothers and sisters, some even contained the smiling face of a child who had died too soon—way too soon. These pictures and words made me intensely nervous. I wanted to leave. What would it mean if she could do exactly as she says?

Then, something miraculous happened. I closed my eyes. Tears began to flow from my eyes, which rarely happened. I imagined my dear friend Scott...his plump cheeks, his fatherly smile...staring at me.

The day he died; he took a part of me with him. I thought to myself, *If Scott comes to visit today, then I will know this is real. I miss him terribly. I wonder if he's okay. Did he forgive me?*

Deb's husband guided me to her office on the second floor of their home. I sat in a white fabric chair that was more comfortable than it looked. It was a formal chair, the kind your mother wouldn't have wanted you to sit in when you were young. Deb sat down in front of me. I thought about eating a Snickers bar—my favorite candy—and to avoid giving her any cues, I kept my 'steely face' on. I thought if I imagined eating a Snickers bar, she wouldn't be able to read my mind.

The truth is, I don't remember a lot after that moment. That's the absolute truth. I had always imagined a bridge between life and death, and that when a person died, they went to another place, or maybe to no place, where they no longer existed. Their form and shape evaporated and became one with the world of death.

However, with every piece of evidence Deb gave me about my dear friend Scott, my imaginary bridge rippled and swayed, and the shield of rationality that contained my haunting fear of death was taken down, one wooden beam at a time, until I was naked in that chair, weeping like a child.

Deb destroyed the bridge I had used to protect the pain of every death and loss I had experienced. Every wooden beam that bridge was made up of was a soul that had died, and I was bound and determined to pretend that I was no longer in pain and had come to accept the loss of these beautiful souls. You see, if the dead are "over there," then they are hidden to us, lost to us. They were in the seeds of new earth, and their energy swirled into the energy of all departed souls.

However, Scott was *here.*

He was speaking through Deb and telling her things only the two of us knew. Every word spoken in the perfect timbre of her confident and compassionate voice rocked my reality of life and death forever. The bridge of life and death was forever destroyed in that moment; I was left weeping in that white chair, knowing that my friend Scott had been there all along. I was without words.

Deb broke the intensity of that moment by asking me, "Would you like some water, Brian...or vodka?" She held up two plastic water bottles, and I accepted one along with some chocolate from the bowl next to me.

Then, she said, "Okay, smart ass. I told you that you're a medium too, and I wasn't joking. Do you want me to prove it?" I nodded my approval, but I also felt more vulnerable than I had ever felt. I was holding my arms around my chest; I was broken open. There was no blanket large enough to contain me.

"Okay. Let's make this easy on you. Take some deep breaths and tell me about an animal I have in this room."

"You mean an animal that has passed?"

"Yes, of course. There are no other animals in here."

"I don't know what you mean. I can't."

"Brian, shut your damn mind and tell me what you feel in the room."

I didn't feel anything, but then I got a flash across my eyes.

"I see a mid-size, brown-haired dog that has a mane like a lion. He feels like a bear to me, and he has a red bandana. He is with you every night. He almost guards you, and he sleeps in your room at the head of the bed, which is not typical. I believe he slept more often with your children, but he is visiting you a lot for some reason."

Deb stepped out of the room and returned with a silver-framed picture of a Chow. The dog had a red bandana around his neck and etched at the bottom of the silver frame was the name "Bear."

"Still think I'm crazy?"

"No, I think I am," I replied.

It would take me almost two years to return to Deb's door for mentoring to become a medium, but I will never forget how that moment changed me forever. The bridge of reason, fear, and having all this life and death stuff figured out died that day. It was very moving and miraculous...and scary as hell.

Resonance.

So much of my growth in life has not been about learning new things. More often, it is unlearning old things. It is almost as if jackets of belief and thought are removed over time because many of my beliefs were formed to cope with the pain and suffering of this life. My ways of coping were often designed to cover up that pain, to pretend it wasn't there. There was a blanket of cynicism and self-hatred that kept me warm—it was familiar. It is not so different from watching a movie multiple times, because somehow, knowing the arc of the journey awaiting me was predictable and fit nicely into the box of my reality.

In those two years, I needed to die. My old self with my old beliefs needed to die. Those two years would almost kill me, because sometimes, being reborn is painful and arduous and lonely as hell.

I guess, for me, this was necessary.

Resonance

The resonance of the wind that destroyed the Tacoma Narrows Bridge on that fateful day was the same wind that shook my world that afternoon in Deb's office.

Over the next two years, the vibrations of that moment would destroy everything I thought I knew about myself and this life. The vibrations of that day would destroy me, transform every cell in my body, and change every thought in my awareness.

Chapter 6

HADES

I asked my first teacher in mediumship one time, "Is animal communication different from mediumship? My friend from the mentoring program told me she's an animal communicator. What's that mean?"

She leaned back in her chair and said, "I won't answer that for you. I have a question for you instead. Does every living thing have a soul?"

The pause made my mind fill with images of every dog and a few cats alone the way, even some guinea pigs.

I replied, "Yes. Of course."

She then said something I would never forget, "Brian, you cannot honor the soul of any animal if you don't love it. If you imagine the human soul to be above any other animal, you will never be able to tell their story. If you imagine your soul above any other person or any other animal, you cannot fully honor their journey because, in your world, you will only see an animal's journey through your imagined dominion."

That's a mouthful. I know. She's clearly smarter than me, but the message she offered gave me permission as a medium to feel into any spirit that came to visit and connect. The door of my work was easily opened by a paw or a beak. That may seem too simple, but, for me, it was important to understand the limitations we create or accept from others will often become beliefs we will prove through our experience.

In other words, if I believe animal communication is not possible through mediumship and there is a different door for that connection, then I will never notice the brilliant spirits with fur, scales, and slime hoping to gain my attention to offer their memories, lessons, and love.

This does not mean animal communication is not a discipline worthy of our time and attention, mediumship is mediumship is mediumship. You can only connect well with a bird if you can differentiate between a parrot and a budgie. You can only support a dog coming through for their family if you understand the difference between a Saint Bernard and a Chihuahua. There is a wisdom and a context that is necessary to ground the evidence to honor the Spirit that has chosen you as their communicator.

However, the beginning of your journey in mediumship should offer an instrument that allows any creatures, great and small.

#

I'd had my own experience with the inexplicable power of animals partnering with your pain and being your mirror. My teacher healer was a horse named Hades. He earned his name, and he earned his purpose.

When going through this training in my master's degree in counseling, a weekend retreat with these miracle workers taught me about a new kind of witness. Hades, a brown 22-year-old draft horse, used and abused by his handlers for years to pull a cart through an old town area in Nebraska, ended up at this rescue in Fort Collins, Colorado.

His hind end showed the scars from the black reins hitting his hide and the deep wound on his neck came from the time the coyotes punctured his neck when he tried to protect a foal. His back right leg also had a puncture wound that became so infected they were certain he wouldn't survive.

Because he was no longer a good draft horse, he was to be offered up as dog food. The rescue intervened at the last minute, and Hades was given his new name to honor his new escape from the underworld.

He'd only been there two weeks when I went to the training. We were told to go into the pen and use our lead to guide our assigned horse to a post where we could then groom them. I watched as the other folks approached their horse and they walked right up and placed the leads, guiding the horse to their post to begin the brushing and stroking.

Hades moved away every time I approached him. He would turn his blue eye covered in a creamy gauze of pink and cream clearly making his visibility challenging at best. I stood there, confused and at a certain point, frustrated as hell. I went sideways slowly, and Hades acted like he didn't see me.

Then, he moved away just in time to avoid me completing the first task. I kept feeling like this wasn't fair because everyone else was already doing the brushing. I was the only idiot who couldn't place the stupid lead on this overgrown obstinate horse from hell. I knew how he'd gotten his name.

He wouldn't do it, and I was afraid I looked like a complete fool. Celeste, our lead trainer and all-around horse whisperer extraordinaire, stood alongside me and said, "Hades doesn't want to come to you."

I'm thinking to myself, Duh! Wow! You're amazing. Clearly not a human whisperer either!

I replied in my professional voice, "No, he doesn't." (With a silent "Bitch, please!" under my breath.)

"Are you angry with him for not doing what you want him to do?" she asked.

I replied in my very very professional voice, "No, he needs to do what he knows is right for him."

She interrupts, "That's not what your energy is saying. It's saying that you are chasing him and he's making you look like a fool! It's been over two hours, and he will not come to you. Why won't Hades come to you?"

I looked at her, and then I was pissed. She clearly didn't know I was a second-year master's level student with straight A's! Who does this bitch think she is?

I replied in my 'not at all professional and full-on sarcastic' voice, "This is stupid! I feel set-up. I don't even like horses, and I got assigned the worst one."

"Do you think we intentionally gave you Hades to piss you off?"

"Yes. It's because I'm the only man so I'm assigned the hardest horse to knock me down a peg or two."

Yup! I too suffer from the nonsense that my privilege causes me to be oppressed. NOT! I'm in full-on baby mode at this point.

Celeste smiled, and said, "Brian, we didn't assign you Hades. He picked you. Remember when we had you stand by the posts, and he walked right to the fence across from you. He chose you. He's just waiting to see if you like him. He won't come over to you until he knows you like him. He's been ordered around his whole life and forced to please angry men with whips and loud voices. He will only come to a person who is soft and wants to love him. Have you ever been abused by someone in power and had your very voice stolen from you?"

"No. Not that I remember," I said.

"Who are you protecting? Him or you?," she said.

"I'm just... I don't know what you want from me."

"Brian, who took your voice?"

"I... a man with a collar!"

Celeste mirrored me in every way, and she replied with the sharpest edges of kindness a sword of clarity could offer as it penetrates through a layer of time to a darkened room in a seminary when I was 12. That memory washed over me, and felt my legs began to shake and tremble. Celeste approached me and I collapsed into her arms, hearing sounds that resembled cries of anguish in heaving sighs of coughs as streams of snot flowed from every nostril.

Spiritual awakenings are nasty at times.

I hate these moments. I felt so cool when I got there, but instead, I'm reduced to tears and being held by a cowgirl far wiser than my thirty-three-year-old self. My degrees and resume and facade all failed me in that moment, and I was just a twelve-year-old boy trying to scream for the first time.

Celeste held me and even rocked me as my tears formed images seen through my mind's eyes a million times in the past rise up and flood my brain. I was peeled away in layers all the way to the twelve-year-old boy floating above my body as I'm being raped below. My voice was lost in the ethers above, and the words to explain the scars placed deep within my skin on those nights never formed sentences. They were moans and whimpers only the song of the wind could harmonize.

I heard my breathing soften and I felt the oxygen returning my eyes to clarity. I watched the dust on the ground below settle in a cloud descending over my New Balance brown hiking shoes that had a waterproof spray and yellow lines of color wrapped around the brown laces that held this moment in place. I kept describing my shoes to myself until her voice found me.

Celeste said quietly, "Brian, look. Turn around very slowly."

I turned around, and Hades was staring right at me. His body was perpendicular to mine. Hades made a circle and returned to me with his head facing mine. I placed my hand directly above his eyes and cried with him. He lowered his head, and I placed the lead around his neck, guiding him around to my post.

Hades had chosen me, but my greatest wounds had chosen him. Hades was my healer, and I was, in some small way, his companion. We had known a different hell, but we had both survived. Mercy was our language, and no one had authority in this dance. The mercy he gave me by choosing me was the mercy I gave him by loving every moment of returning the grace offered to me.

As I gently used the brush and made circular motions on his sides, he looked uncomfortable with me until my strokes joined the movement of hair the wind honored. The paths the wind carved into his lines of hair became my guide. He then looked at me with softness and joy. He knew I loved him, and I knew he loved me.

On the last day, I was working with his feet, and I could feel the ridge where the deep wound became infected in his leg. It was still healing as a yellow ooze still poured from the site. I softened my breath, and I placed my hand against this place, hearing a soft moan. He made no motion to move his leg in any way and I knew he felt the warmth and the love I poured into him.

We were both wounded, and we both had scars that required regular debriding and cleaning.

Hades was my guide across my river Styx. I had a space inside me where the pain had been replaced with a void. I felt space and I could breathe in new ways again. The clench of that history softened more and more in his gauze-filled blue eyes. He softened as I softened. His breath expanded as my soul did. We were two souls seeking ground and found a safe reprieve in the other, a witness. Some might say the eyes of mercy connected us both.

Moments of that dark room at the seminary on South Cherry Street in Glendale, Colorado no longer exist in my memory. I can't construct bridges between images any longer. Something was left behind in that dusty corral.

#

"Brian, can you please come tonight? I'd forgotten to tell you two days prior. It's been chaotic lately. I know you understand." Julie's voice quakes like a wave through the lines of text that flash onto my phone. I can feel the urgency and the vulnerability wrap around every word that appears.

The new text appears, and her imaginary voice fills my ears again: "Brian, we need you to help us say goodbye to Cody. It's time. His legs are making it clear that it is time."

Julie is this long wavy-haired natural redhead that feels like the sister and mother everyone wishes they had. We never chose our friendship; it was simply there. She never fails at being there when I need her, so any request is never a question. It is always "How?"

The Animal Assisted Therapy Program of Colorado is an amazing non-profit that provides powerful therapy to clients in different forests of grief, especially children. They have everything from horses to goats (the big ones that stand on their hind legs and lean against you while chewing on your clothes), cats, Pygmy goats, bunnies, and mice. I know there's more, but let's just say it is a different kind of ark. This Ark is a group of powerful women, and the flood is traumatic moments held in moments of time repeating images where powerlessness leads to hopelessness.

These angels' journey into the memories of these floods and offer a witness that quiets the chaotic rhythms of cortisol and fear.

Julie's text glowed brightly on the dark basement couch where my day with a nasty headache had reduced me to Netflix and Cheetos. But I knew this was one I couldn't ignore. The legs of horses are often the decision makers of knowing when mercy is the only appropriate medicine. When this becomes clear due to a hip issue, knee problems, or a deep split in the bone of the hoof no farrier can heal, the humans then need to set a timeline for mercy to be their final gift.

These animals are healers. I don't believe this designation is limited to this unique band of healers, but I do know these animals on this little ranch are co-therapists in the truest sense. There are times when the therapist is guiding the client, and more often, it is the furry souls directing the work of therapy down unknown trails and forests known only to their wise instinct.

As I arrived, I was led to Cody immediately. As I stood and placed my hand on Cody, I was feeling completely inadequate and so confused about how to approach a moment like this one. The air is familiar. It is the time when Death has joined us, and we accept her presence.

She's not here to shock us today or fill us with horror. She will be the gentle hand to guide Cody into peace. Death was invited and her breath stills our voices and makes us cautious with our words.

As I feel Cody lean a bit closer to me, his eyes catch mine. He knew before we saw one another that I was a friend. Horses know these things. Then, in a wave of energy, a man appears. A taller man with a large belt buckle and jeans with a long sleeve striped shirt stands on the other side of this large brown horse and looks like a force of light moving his hands along his mane and gently making circles behind his ears.

"Please let them know I will be there to receive Cody. Cody walked me through my sorrows, and I am honored to greet him as he says goodbye to all of you."

As I shared the image and the words, more information begins to flow through. I seldom remember the rest of the reading. I'm not going into some deep trance, but my hands move and the information is in front of me somehow. I am watching the information cross my lips, but the wholeness of the thoughts is not there. They don't belong to me, and it isn't for me. It is being on the back end of a moving wave, and I trust the gentle guidance these souls offer in moments like these.

This volunteer in spirit had died from cancer and was very close to Cody. His presence gave the intended message of trust and acceptance the staff needed.

What I never shared was when Hades' blue eyes met mine. I saw his eyes at the end, and I knew he was also there. Hades' spirit joined me at the gate and guided me with every exchange.

Hades was leading me out of the darkness and across a river that had held me in its rapids for many seasons, and his blue eyes were the promise of the witness. When another soul witnesses our suffering, our grief is transformed.

Chapter 7

THE WEIGHT OF WIND

At the ripe age of twenty-one, having a stethoscope around my neck made me feel accomplished and powerful, even though I had no formal medical training in any way.

Two weeks prior, the team at the Korr Mission in the middle of the Kaisut Desert in Kenya had gotten their wires crossed with the agency where I was volunteering. They thought they were receiving a medical student, but instead, they got me - bachelor's degree with no real practical world skills to share.

We both felt betrayed, but Sister Naferi insisted we make this experience a meaningful one. At the medical clinic, the first skill she taught me was to listen to the lobes of the lungs.

As she asked people to take a deep breath, she said, "Do you hear the wind on a gentle summer's day or do you hear a storm coming with the sounds of distant thunder?" A young boy named Abraham carried his spear into the exam room, and he stared ahead, not making eye contact. Sister Naferi changed the dressings on his back, the result of being attacked by a real-life lion while herding the goats. The wounds had yellow pus oozing in one of the stripes that etched deep into his back, but the other channels had healed.

She said, "Daniel, it looks like we need another antibiotic shot. Do you agree?"

Daniel nodded but his eyes remained fixed on the wall across from him. He was likely no more than eight years old, but he had a countenance and focus that surprised me. In the Samburu tribe, he was expected to hunt for ostrich eggs while ensuring the herd of goats were guided to vegetation in the desert to keep their greatest assets in healthy shape.

As she plunged the shot into his hip, she looked at me with a nod to let me know it was time for me to do my one job. She said, "Kupumua, Daniel!" She spoke Kiswahili instead of the native tongue, but he responded as I placed the stethoscope on his back. I started with the upper quadrants, and the wind was a summer breeze. As I dropped to the lowest quadrant, the wind was ragged and sounded like a pencil scratching deep into lined paper when I was learning to write letters on countless worksheets.

She placed the used needle in a blue antiseptic jar, and she asked, "Do you hear something?"

I replied, "It's a storm but it sounds like crumpled paper. It sounds that way in every quadrant. Do you agree?"

I kept the stethoscope placed on the middle of his back and handed her the ears.

"Brian, good work! He's got asthma. Do you know what this is?" My mother and brother had severe asthma, so I knew this only too well. She tapped on his back and listened more intently. She then handed him some small white tablets in a small plastic bag.

In that moment, as he exited the room, I looked at her and recognized this volunteer journey had little to do with helping anyone. I was a student and everyone around me were teachers, far wiser and more mature. I was still enamored with my drama to a crippling degree at times, and I saw the highs and lows of my story as verses instead of a chorus. I only had one week left before I was to be sent back to Nairobi to wait for a new placement.

Sister Naferi said, "Tomorrow, we visit a local village and basically bring the medical clinic to our outlying communities. I could really use your help if you're willing to join us." I knew I had little to offer to the real work, but I learned so much from her. She had this artful way of protecting my dignity and ensuring I had a way to feel connected to the greater mission.

The Land Rover with the red plus sign on it made us look official, but the empty rivers looked like silver stripes across the barren landscape. "You know, Brian, the Samburu follow the rains with the elephants. It's the arid season, so we likely won't see any elephants today, but the lions are getting hungry. Always watch for the vultures to ensure we don't ever get too close to a fresh kill. The predators will see you as a threat." This felt like wisdom that worked in a gay dance club too.

Before we exited the dust-covered Range Rover with the emergency stripes on our side, Sister Naferi said, "Brian, you'll stay right by my side when we get set-up today. I'll have you distribute the milk powder to the mothers."

I replied, "Yes. Am I checking lungs today?"

"Not today. This medical clinic is completely focused on mothers and their newborns. We meet once a month and we check the weights of babies to see how they are progressing. We also take extra time with brand new babies to get their yellow cards established and begin to track HIV infection rates."

"Sister Naferi, I don't understand. How can we test for HIV? From what I understand, there are no tests available."

"Brian, these yellow cards tell a story." I watched as her head moved and swayed side to side in what I came to see as a uniquely Indian style of non-verbal expression. She then tsked as she looked to her hands. My eyes followed, and the yellow booklets covered in plastic reflected the morning heat of the desert sun. She then said, "You see, the yellow cards will reveal if a baby has HIV.

At 18 months, you will typically see all the babies grow along the black line to show their weight is aligned with their months on this planet. However, if a baby has HIV which they typically get from a mother's breast milk, the baby's weight will fall dramatically off the curve, and they will typically have less than two months to live. Today, we will know which of these babies has HIV and equally important, we will know which of our mothers has HIV."

I replied, "I'm not trying to be challenging here, but we have no medicines in any way for HIV. How does this information help us?"

Sister Naferi responded after licking her sun-parched fingers and running them through her eyebrows. Whenever any of us asked her a question she didn't know how to answer, she'd always pause while grooming herself in this peculiar way.

She then said, "You will see today. We provide the mothers with the babies with HIV calcium tablets and then, at the end, we will pray with them."

As we got out of the truck, the gravity of this medical clinic weighed on me. The other clinics had simply asked me to put on a stethoscope and listen to people's lung chambers to ascertain if they had pneumonia or sometimes, asthma. The crinkled sound of paper in children's lungs always gave away the presence of asthma, but there were no powerful inhalers or medicines to offer. We simply tracked if they needed an antibiotic to address how their asthma predisposed kids to lung infections.

Today was a different day entirely. Today, we were meeting Death and acknowledging defeat with calcium tablets.

The Kaisut Desert in Kenya near the border of Ethiopia was a cruel place but the Samburu and Rendele tribes had existed here for thousands of years. Every single plant that finds a way to grow in these conditions has thorns and all of our work is accomplished in the early morning or late afternoon hours. Over forty mothers, holding babies wrapped in fabric close to their chests where some are holding the hands of other children. As they filled the large plastic Jerry cans they had removed from their backs using the large community well, their yellow cards were held above them in waiting hands, flicking in the wind. Some held the hands of other children who assisted with managing the plastic watering jugs. My mind saw a field of sunflowers in the fall as those yellow cards gently moved side to side in the wind.

The scale we used looked like a produce scale; to the metal arm below the large dial that indicated the weight, Sister Naferi took a large piece of fabric and tied a small hammock to receive the babies. One by one, she placed the babies into the hammock and released them into the fabric cradle. Then, as I recorded the weight, I then plotted the weight on the graph, marking a small "x" to align with their number of months.

We were halfway through, and then I heard Sister Naferi's voice get quiet as she whispered the weight and the months to me. I recorded the weight on the table, and I then placed the "X" on the graph. The "X" was well below the line, and then she said, "Please hold the baby while I take the mother aside." The little girl stared at me with her gleaming eyes, and she looked significantly smaller than any baby we had weighed. The little girl soon fell asleep in my arms with her neck resting on my arm, and I gently rocked her back and forth.

The woman next in line with her son resting in the sun was wiping away the horse flies from his face as she caught my eyes.

She said, "Ukimwi."

I replied, "Ndio." In those two words, we had a complete conversation about life and death.

I stared back at the little girl in my arms and watched her lungs rise and fall with her breaths and felt powerless. If I'm honest, I thought, *What the hell am I doing here?* HIV, the same virus that stole so many of the smiles from my world, was the same particle smaller than a micron that would quiet this little life far too soon.

Sister Naferi said, "I don't see the tablets. I'll be right back." She looked at the next mother in line and placed her hand on her heart to acknowledge the frustration at the wait this had created.

I looked at that scale, and I realized it was measuring so much more than weight. Life was on the line as was every mother with her baby wrapped in beautiful colored fabrics. If a baby had the virus, the mother standing across from me was also infected. I placed the baby against my chest with one arm and began to rock her. She smiled with glee, but I could tell she was not well. Her frame was smaller, and her lungs rose like spires against her skin every time she exhaled.

I kept thinking the movement and the purposeful scurry of this event would stop and everyone would scream to the sky, demanding an explanation. However, the nuns were organizing their stations, checking eyesight in the toddlers present, and another sister was assisting the mothers in her line with the bags of corn and beans.

The line of women with large plastic Jerry cans with random letters and numbers were still waiting for Angelica, the youngest sister in the convent, to manually raise and lower the red pump handle to fill each ten-gallon container. She was struggling with the metallic rod that went through the handle, securing it when it is not attended.

The mother of the baby in my arms used her fabric dress to slap the horse flies that kept landing on her cheeks as I watched the weight of Sister Naferi's words land as punches. Sister Naferi then placed her left hand on the mother's shoulder and placed her right hand on her chest as they dropped their heads in prayer.

This operation kept moving, but the world in this baby's eyes now had a different schedule. I stared at her, and I knew that God was an evil son of a bitch. We could offer them prayers and Calcium tablets, which was like offering a band-aid to a gunshot victim. Somehow, giving something to these mothers with babies in their arms soon to die made us feel better, even though we knew it was a hopeless situation.

Sister Naferi returned to the front of the line with the mother, and she gripped her hands, offering her a small bag of Calcium tablets. The mother reached for her baby, and I gently placed her back in her arms. She adjusted and placed her baby into the hammock her magical fabric dress created. The mother and her older daughter grabbed their bags of food and off they traveled into an uncertain and cruel future of profound grief.

We began to weigh the babies once again. Two more babies would be off the curve, and two more times, I held the baby as the mother was pulled aside for a discussion and a hands-on prayer. The faces of these mothers were not just hearing their child's death sentence; they were also being given their own. The instinct of every mother was to comfort their child, and witnessing these moments has never become less potent.

As we drove back to the Korr Mission, I was angry. I sulked in the back of the Land Rover and stared out the window, watching the sand rise in clouds. The afternoon light painted them orange and red but there was nothing my eyes could see as beautiful. The other sisters ignored me because I was clearly not engaging with their gentle salutations. We even got to see giraffes eating leaves off acacia trees and ostrich cruising by faster than our vehicle.

Sister Naferi sat in the passenger seat, and she looked in the rearview mirror as she said, "Brian, today was hard. Wasn't it?"

I replied simply, "Yes."

"Thank goodness God carries our burdens. Do you let God carry your burdens?"

I paused and felt the bitterness of my anger rise, and I said, "God must be cruel. How could God allow this to happen?"

A silence fell across the truck as Sister Naferi turned around from the front and met my eyes. Her fingers pushed through the wild hairs of her eyebrows demanding they obey the path her wet finger created.

She finally replied, "God loves you, Brian. This I know, my dear one. You've got a God problem."

I replied curtly, saying, "I don't need God's support. How about, instead, God reach to the dying children and these very ill mothers? What about them?"

The word "God" was one that often shut me down. I had seen many men with white collars tell me of God's love as they either judged or deeply wounded me in the dark. Parts of me were still lost in dark rooms that were supposed to be sacred, and I wanted nothing to do with that God.

Sister Naferi said, "Oh, my Dear One. You are angry because you love. You are angry because life is unfair. You are angry, because there is suffering, we cannot fix? Is that right?"

I replied, "Yes! Exactly!"

She replied, "When my brother died, I was only nine years old. He was thirteen at the time, and our neighbors in our village carried his body back to us. His lifeless body was placed on the ground in the center of our home. I watched as my mother wept. My mother and her sister cleaned his body and she kissed him. My father stayed outside and smoked his cigarettes. I could hear his muffled cries, but my brother was dead. I wanted to die too, Brian. Do you know this feeling? I know you do."

"Yes."

"I was angry with God. He took my protector and my dearest friend. I was angry for many years, Brian. We cannot rush these things. Grief is our greatest teacher about God. Did you know that?"

As every word from her mouth filled the quiet Land Rover, my anger was softening into something else. I don't have words for this 'between space' where the harbors of anger no longer grip my chest and cause my fists to clench.

She then said words that would work on me for the rest of my life.

"Brian, your anger isn't real, but your heartbreak is. God can carry all of this. Did you know that? God must be a familiar face we see as family, or a prayer is another's words with no feeling. God is in the feelings. Do you know what I mean?"

I said, "Yes", but if I'm honest, I had no clue what she meant at the time.

She continued, saying, "Rather than feeling sorry for these mothers, we must learn from them. When I pray with these mothers, you likely notice my left hand reaching out as I place my right hand on their heart. I imagine my brother's hand in mine because he was always my greatest example of love. I reach for him as I pray with these mothers or with anyone. You may not believe me, but there are moments when I feel his hand in mine. Who have you lost in life that you are not yet reaching to?"

"Are you saying your brother is your God," I asked.

"I'm saying my brother is the person I knew loved me and I saw the love and grace in his eyes I needed on my hardest of days. My brother taught me that God is in all of us, and it is my job to see through those eyes. In those arms, watching you hold those babies, I saw you being the eyes of God for that moment. We are all God, and God is all of us. Does that make sense?"

"Yes, I think I do," I replied.

Sister Naferi reached out her hands to all of us in the back of the truck. She placed her left hand out and her right hand on her heart.

She said, "See him in every situation, because he is there. Feel him in every moment because he is there. Reach to him when you cannot stand up to the circumstances of life. Know he is there. Does this make sense, dear one?"

I felt the tears roll down my face, but I held back the tears. Then, I felt a warm tingle on my chest, and it spread across my entire body. I will never forget that night when I traded my anger and allowed the grace to touch the brokenness.

I've needed to be reminded to reach out with my hand on my heart and allow the grace that has never failed me to comfort me, anchor me, and guide me.

My challenges in mediumship are always a God problem. I'll tell you it's about my health, my stress level, my lack of support, my bank account, but it's always a God problem. Do I have the presence of mind to remember the moment when the grace touched the broken parts and reminded me the soft energy of love reaches to every soul in their greatest desperation? As a medium, I am only asked to trust and open my heart to the vulnerability of the work. Spirit always does the rest.

Sister Naferi looked straight forward as the lights of the Land Rover bounced with the undulating waves of the dark desert night. She asked, "Brian, do you remember what I taught you when listening to your lungs?"

I replied, "Yes. It was my first skill."

She then said, "Do you hear the wind on a gentle summer's day, or do you hear a storm coming with the sounds of distant thunder? Regardless of the impending weather, God is the light we cannot always see, but we can always feel. There is a moment when we trust the weather and we honor every lesson her skies offer. Do you trust this, Brian? Do you trust you are carried through any storm?"

Yes, Sister Naferi. I finally trust this grace. Thank you.

Chapter 8

AN UNCOMMON GRACE

Peggy Martin was always the speaker at the local AA conference I couldn't wait to hear. I'd be in my seat and couldn't wait for her words to save me for another day. This particular AA event was called the Cornhusker Roundup in Omaha, Nebraska. The cornfields of Nebraska is where I found out that hope was an action, and in my college career at a Catholic university, I discovered cowboys are great kissers and there's a reason sheep are so happy.

I ended up here after destroying myself in multiple ways in Washington DC and my mom and dad hoped that pesky gay thing would remain on the east coast as I began my third year of college in Nebraska. My version of living was jumping from one chaos to the next. Wherever I write chaos, insert boys. Don't judge. It will work for many of you too.

Here I was on a Saturday morning no less, sitting and waiting to hear one of my heroes Peggy Martin speak to the heart of me at an AA twelve-step conference. So, I guess you can infer that Nebraska, with farmers and moonshine, didn't offer the solace of fields and meadows Willa Cather had promised. Instead, dusty streets and X-rated stores across the Iowa border led me to new ways of giving away my dignity in the arms of cigarette-fueled cowboys. It all sounds so romantic, but this period of life taught me that certain stains never fully escape the forgetfulness of time. When you have nothing to protect, you have a gate that has no latch. The penetrations of the dark from my childhood with a man and another with a collar opened a gate to my person that I had not even the slightest awareness of how to close. Frankly, I didn't even know it was open.

I had a major life problem, and a group of gay men seeking sobriety found me in the rivers of my fear and offered not only a life raft but a sense of belonging I sought in every corner of my life. It was a belonging I didn't trust for a long time, but that love that reached to me found ways inside the brokenness and stories of self-hatred that felt like reality. I now know that darkness was the fantasy, and the reality was the love.

Peggy walked up to that lectern and she did not disappoint. She told the same stories with a few additions. She explained her journey in France where she befriended a 'lady of the night' as she called her. Peg described in excruciating detail the moments of urine-soaked bedding and haunted cries from this lost soul as Peggy held her hands. After visiting her for a time, this woman became sicker and sicker, but Peggy kept the commitment to be with her. As Peggy's drinking went out of control, she saw the mirror of herself in this woman, slowly dying in a dingy room. Peggy would always tear up and relive that haunted moment with her death, trusting that the story would carve a possibility of hope in any lucky enough to hear it.

Peggy said, "We are all butterflies, and our wings are glued to the pavement. Cars and trucks whisk by, and our wings are just not free to escape the chaos and the fear that defines every moment. Do you know that place, my friends?"

I looked around and I saw the tears and the nods that made us all One for that sixty-minute talk. Every person understood that moment of desperately wanting to spread our wings but being glued to the pavement.

After her talk, there was always a large group of folks surrounding her and hoping to catch the smile of such a sincere mirror. I started to walk out of the room, and my sponsor, Scott Jackman, said, "Did you thank the speaker?" I hated when Momma Jackman would catch me and then ask that I politely keep my promise. I gave him the biggest eye roll I could muster and I'm certain a sigh to match as I turned on my heel to go thank the stupid speaker that had changed my life.

As I stood behind the line of people, Peggy said loudly, "Okay, the next speaker is about to start. Thank you for your kind words." Yes! I can avoid making eye contact with another human. As I was walking back to my seat, Peggy caught up with me, "Can you and I sit in the lobby for a chat?"

I replied with my infamous I don't what else to say reply, "Yup."

As I sat across from her, she asked, "Brian, I watched you during my talk today. I bet we have a lot in common."

"Yup," I replied. At this point, she likely thought I was touched.

Peggy said, "tell me how it's going with your sobriety. Scott and I had a chat recently. Congrats on your one-year coin by the way. He tells me you're not sure alcohol is the real issue."

I replied, "That's right. I know I'm crazy, but if I'm honest, I never drank to excess. Even, drugs were used sparingly, and typically, it was to distract myself from doing crazy stuff. I just feel things so deeply and I feel so misunderstood. Life is profoundly unfair. Do you know what I mean?"

Peggy leaned forward with a look of concern and presence I had seldom encountered in others. She then asked, "Are you fair with life? Are you asking for something you're not giving?"

I replied, "I guess. I'm doing my fourth step in a couple of weeks. Scott says I will have new eyes, whatever that means."

Peggy added, "Brian, I'm also in Alanon. To be honest, you don't seem like an alcoholic. Instead of being addicted to alcohol, you're addicted to your pain. Do you still imagine your life is harder than everyone else?"

I felt this anger rise in me, but I wanted her to like me. I tried to find some inner words that would be an antacid for my emotion. I said, "Peggy, you're not gay. You wouldn't get it. I've had so many friends die from AIDS and I've been bullied for simply being who God made me."

Peggy replied, "Honey, I know your pain. I'm not in your shoes, but I know that pain of being completely alone and misunderstood. Don't you think the heartbreaks of every other person in this conference hall want desperately to be heard? We don't have the luxury of comparing our pain because that can be all the excuse, we need to destroy ourselves. I decided one day that pain is pain. Your pain matters to me, Honey. It wasn't until my pain joined the pain of every other person I met that I really found peace."

Every neuron inside me relaxed in a way I didn't know possible. I wanted to climb into her lap and have her hold me. I said, "Peggy, how did you learn this lesson? I'm an empath, so I find crowds hard at times. I get overwhelmed by people and want to be invisible a lot of the time. Do you know what I mean?"

Peggy looked more intently in my eyes than she ever had, and she said, "Brian, being an empath is a calling to love. Don't you know that? Your empathy is a gift from God, and it is teaching you to love every soul you encounter."

"I have no idea how to live that way. People scare me," I said.

Peggy took my face in her hands, and she said, "Honey, I know this won't make sense to the mind you have in this moment. I am speaking to the future version of you to say, 'I told you so.' As an empath, we can either drown in the stories we marinate the world in or we can use that gift of compassion to love the world. I'm not promising the world will love you back. Have you ever heard of that Jesus fella? He was kind of an expert in this."

I asked, "So, you just want me to love the world? And then, all will be better?"

I felt her hands grip my cheeks even more tightly praying I would hear, saying, "Yes. No one can hurt you when you love them. It's that kind of love that asks for nothing in return and finds joy in the courageous stories' others carry in their heart."

"I love the idea of this. It sounds great, but you haven't met my family," I replied.

Peggy relaxed her hands at her waist, but her eyes stared past my irises into the light of my being. I've only met two people in this life that know how to do this. Peggy was the first.

She continued, saying, "Brian, try this for me. Before you continue the story of how you had the worst parents of all time, I want you to just for a moment wonder about this: What terrifies your mother? How did the world hurt your mother before she became your mother? When you care as much about her pain as your own, you will begin to heal in ways you never imagined."

I began to cry even as the question hit my heart. Peggy joined me. This looked like the final scene from Harold and Maude to anyone observing this moment between this sixty-year-old guru with flats and me, a twenty-year-old in desperate need of some heels.

Peggy pulled me close and rocked me. She then said, "Honey, our mothers are as frightened as we are, if not more so. That energy is what grace feels like. When it hits my heart, I cannot help but cry. The angry mind hates it, because the battles we are always fighting to win against our oppressors don't work when we recognize we are all in cages. Are you ready to be free?"

I pulled back and saw her tears stream down her face. She was weeping for a mother she'd never known and teaching me to love her story and respect her journey in this life. She gave me new eyes and the Grace that holds all of us restored my heart. I said, "Peggy, I'm embarrassed to admit that I have never allowed her pain to matter. Her father died when she was very young, and she has never felt okay in the world since that event."

Peggy held my hands in hers and said, "Brian, you're getting it. We are all empaths by the way. However, an empath can be incredibly dangerous when they only care about their own story. They will demand everyone else be loyal to their pain. Sound familiar?"

I replied, simply, "Yup."

Yup.

She stood up and this ten-minute conversation would reverberate against the walls of my mind as the battle for my pain and the wisdom of Grace would take the front seat of my mind.

My pain demands that seat.

Grace must be invited.

Peggy's final words to me were, "God loves you, Brian. I must say she's got good taste. Whether you have a drinking problem or a thinking problem, the answer is the same: Love well. No matter the obstacles, love anyway. I know that sounds like a twenty-five-cent bumper sticker, but it's the truth that will never be shaken. The eyes you offer another's pain will always be the emergency exit for your own. Most empathic people drown in a pool of their own making, but few souls really know the love that soars to the heavens. Maybe, yours is an ocean."

Peggy cackled; and even weirder, I joined her. I was beginning to see just how wise her words were, and I laughed for real. That was a feeling I had not felt in many years. Peggy continued, saying, "It all begins with Love that asks for nothing in return. By the way, it ends with that too. If you're lucky enough to love in this way, you will be blessed to know the face of grief. However, that's a lesson for another time."

I never had another moment with Peggy in that special way. The lesson she offered me has been one that revisits me when I need it most. I recognized soon after that I did not have a drinking problem, but it was clear the gifts of the twelve steps and the sense of belonging offered at that time continues to save my life.

When my mother died, I often pictured her and Peggy having time together. I prayed for this reunion of two powerful and courageous women who never met in life. I love to believe that, in death, everyone sees the similarities of lessons throughout their time here. There is no sense of separation or feeling of being isolated. There is no lesson that is not ours. There is no story that has villains and victims and heroes. Instead, the plot is shared and the lesson universal.

I now understand she was one of my first teachers in mediumship. I still place my demanding angry child in the driver's seat, and it always leads me to the same place. I still act bemused and forlorn at times, but then, Peggy's Spirit will once again invite me to remember the day when Grace winked at me for the first time.

Chapter 9

WHEN NAPOLEON WAS DEFEATED BY THE GREAT TAPPER

"Spotlight", the Academy Award-winning movie from 2015, seemed like a nice art house movie that would make me feel like I earned my NPR (National Public Radio) cred while inhaling extra buttery popcorn with Hot Tamales and Sour Skittles. I am a junk food afficionado. I have never met something made with sugar that I didn't happily devour.

So, as I walked into the lovely theater with a largely white-haired retired crowd discussing climate change and why matinee prices had traveled over $10 a ticket, I texted John to let him know I was seeing "Spotlight." I thought the movie was about Watergate and the role Woodward and Bernstein played in the demise of Nixon.

John wrote back, "Don't eat too much candy. You always feel like crap when you eat too much." I wrote back, "Don't worry. In New York, they only sell bite-sized candies similar to Halloween."

I lied as my extra-large theater sized candies sat on my lap.

Strike One of My Karmic Takedown!

Then, John texted, asking, "Don't you have your workshop all day?" I replied, "Nope. They let us out early.

Strike Two!

John then wrote, "By the way, Spotlight is not about Watergate. It's about the Catholic priests sexually abusing children in Boston and the massive investigation performed by a team of reporters that proved this kind of abuse is systemic."

Oh crap.

Then, the lights dimmed. My butt spent five minutes trying to find some loft until I finally accepted the inevitable twenty-year old butt print as defined as a fossil where every other ticket holder for twenty years or more eventually surrendered.

Then, strike three was just about to occur.

An older woman with a red wig that needed some major adjustments turned around and said, "Sir! Sir! Can you please stop tapping? It's annoying." I didn't even have time to respond. She continued as she stared at her husband next to her who was then wiping his glasses and trying to pretend he was deaf. "Harold! Can you ask this man behind you to stop tapping?"

Harold looked up but not at her and said exactly what I wanted to say, "Lois, what? What's the problem?"

She continued, "He is tapping and tapping and tapping, I can't pay attention to my own thoughts. He is a super tapper."

Harold looked down at this point, and now I was enjoying the entire scene. Harold finally looked at her with his newly cleaned glasses, and he said, "Lois, that was me. I'm sorry. I can't get that damn song out of my head. You know, the one in the cab where the... the guy singer from the seventies but with his piano?"

Lois replied, "You mean the piano man?"

Harold replied, "Yes! It's that piano man!"

Lois said, "His name is not 'Piano Man.' His name is Elton Joel."

Harold said, "No no no no. That's crazy. It's Elton John."

She yelled out, "That's what I said! Billy Joel!"

Harold said, "Yes! That's it. You've got it. Billy Elton. He's why I'm tapping."

Lois looked forward and said, "Well, stop the damn tapping! Please! I can't take it!"

Harold looked down and soon, the snoring started. It was halfway through the third preview when the third Merchant and Ivory film featuring very unhappy privileged white people in corsets and top hats looking sullen and very sincere about the matter at hand that I could not care one tiny fifth of a nanosecond about let us know their film was soon to arrive to theaters everywhere. I laughed on the inside and decided to see if loud popcorn chewing would drive Lois over the edge. How would snoring and loud machination noises impact her mental state?

Strike Three!

To my surprise, Lois looked at that screen as if the second coming of Christ or Billy Elton himself would magically break into song at any moment.

Finally, the movie started.

My inner movie started on an old reel inside of me that had no PAUSE button. I was riveted and trapped observing two stories at once and they formed a perfect union to challenge the ways in which this pain didn't matter. This pain was historic and had no impact on me today. This pain was the Richter scale I fought to keep at a manageable level to protect the citizens in my small village of life. If this pain was to speak, my foundation would crumble and damage many I love in the wake of after-shocks.

Yelp.

I felt the gravity of each passing moment in that film press on the disks in my cervical region first until the vertebral spaces were densely packed. Then, the thoracic region descended as the smaller muscles that grab onto the spine and the scapula are trying to keep this spine from bowing so they begin to spasm. I stretch out and try to get my body to calm the fuck down. Then, my hips started to scream with pain as the nerve pain I knew well traveled down my right leg and lit up my calf muscle and the top of my foot. As the story advanced and the abused spoke their truth while reporters looked on with disgust and empathy, I felt as if their eyes were meeting mine.

Then, at some point, the movie disappeared completely from view. I was in a room at a seminary my parents had me visit on the weekend to spend time with the loved-by-all head priest. His charisma and presence made him a favorite in the community, and I loved him. But then, the moments when the priest over six feet tall in green and black plaid boxers with a white undershirt making me an apple cider mix drink began the journey into losing my dignity.

The images of him standing above me, putting mousse in my hair while laughing, the fondling, the warm mouth we use to show we love one another, the eyes growing heavy, the sharp pains in my diaphragm that made the air too hot to breathe, and the holding with kisses on my neck as my fight for eyes to stay open failed me. I surrendered for the love. This brutal exchange felt fair to my younger mind.

The morning became the ritual where pretending was a game. I became so good that I always lost this game. My voice became so distant, and I could feel myself dividing into two.

I was eleven or twelve.

I was a difficult kid.

I deserved the ritual, but I wasn't sure it was real.

I was a good liar and I was certain this was just me wanting attention again.

I didn't want to lose his love. He did love me, right?

Love.
Darkness.
Holding. Comforting me. Safe again.
Pain. Sharp.
AGONY!!!!

Quiet.

Agony can be the quietest sound across the landscape of a person's body. Anguish is silent.
You can be on fire, and no one can see.
You can be frozen, and the sun won't notice.
You can be loud but be filled with hollow words.

"Brian, what happened? Why do you have blood and mucous in your underwear?" my mother asked one day. She held my underwear in her hands, and I kept waiting for her to connect all the dots, but I saw the two of us choose to remain confused.

I was shocked and naked and embarrassed and ashamed and afraid and frozen. I could get my body and mouth to do things when I froze. He was the puppeteer, and I was no longer a real boy.

My mom said again, "Brian, have you been having stomach pains? Can you tell me when this started to occur?"

"I don't know," I said. My mind grabbed for memories, but they faded like snow on your tongue. I could taste and feel the chill, but then it was gone.

I don't know. I really don't know.

I know now. I'm lying. I know exactly what happened.

"Mr. Bowles, we will need to do a flexible sigmoidoscopy. It's where we place a camera inside you to assess just how serious this is."

The gastroenterologist then looked very concerned and said, "You have blood in your rectum, young man. Are you experiencing pain?"

Yes. It's an earthquake.

I looked forward and thought I said, "Sure."

I must not have found the voice, so my silence caused him to raise his voice, saying, "You have blood in your rectum, young man. We need to find out why. Does that make sense?"

I replied with actual words as if I was responding for someone else. "Sure."

I have blood in my rectum.

Knives at night attacking the defenseless temple with a child on the altar sacrificing...

Don't be so dramatic. It's not what happened.

Knives cutting into my flesh.

Screaming in agony as the scope with a sharp metal claw took samples and vomit flying from my mouth as blood appeared in the metallic kidney-shaped bowl the nurse who never said her name or looked at me held below as I thought my stomach would explode out of me as I waited for the ground to return beneath my feet but it never did.

"Brian has ulcerative colitis. He likely has the same stomach issues my sister had when she was younger," my mom said at the dinner table as the pasta looked alive on my plate. The snakes were going to finally complete the job and devour me. I was dying, but I was trying to look alive everywhere I went. I was sitting there, but my mom was using my name. Had I become that invisible?

My dad woke me up one morning, and said, "Son, you need to take the Sulfasalazine. I know it's a lot and the pills are large, but the doctor says it's either this or daily enemas. Which is it, Son?"

I pushed down the horse pills at six a pop twice a day.

Purple stool and the sharp pangs still screamed, but I became quieter on my western front.

"I'm fine, Mom. Please stop asking."

"Are you sure, Brian? I need to ensure you're okay. The doctor said it can be serious if it is not treated."

"Mom, I'm okay." I am. I am. I am okay. I am. I really am. I am. I am okay. I am. I really am. I am okay. I am okay. I am o-fucking-kay. I am so fucking o-God Damn- kay!!!!!! I am okay!!!!"

My mom said, "I'm so glad you're okay. I was worried. You really had me worried."

"Mom, please don't worry. I'm okay."

"Oh Brian, thank goodness. I don't have to worry."

"No Mom, you have nothing to worry about. I'm okay."

I'm okay.

I'm going to be okay. I will be okay. I need to call John. He's teaching but I need to try. I need to hear his voice. But I'm okay. The blue door on the stall was locked shut, and I was shaking. The diarrhea finally stopped, but the sharp pains continued. The shaking wouldn't stop. I was unravelling.

I couldn't stop, and I was going to burst.
I can't burst here. The building will collapse.
I need to get outside. The sky. The trees.
Dialing
Ring
Ring.....Please
Ring.... Please answer!!!!
Ring
"Brian, how's your trip? I'm about to go...."

His voice. The seismic shift happened as I walked down a street in New York City only able to see the sidewalk and track my progress. My peripheral vision was fading and the lines of concrete became my footprints in the snow.

His voice had eyes and he could see..

I was a racehorse losing again when the bets of expectations were high.

The paper bets fell to the ground as....
"Brian, are you there?"
He heard me. I wasn't silent. The sound escaped.

I tried to, but words pulled apart

no glue

thoughts

separating

cold

hot sky

"John, I..."

"Baby, what's wrong? Are you okay? It's okay, Love. I'm here. I'm here."

John was here.

I could feel him.

The forces of voice to reach across wires hundreds of miles apart, but his voice was pulling the pieces back to when words flew straight

waves against poles

over the Mississipi

through Oklahoma

Kansas Border

Colorado Home Almost

Pueblo

Mountains

Sky

Valleys

Mile High

Littleton

C-470

Mineral Road

Middle School Campus

Second Floor

Team Burgundy

Seventh Grade

After School

Two Hours Earlier

2:35 P.M.

How long before class? Kids coming. Protect them, John.

Please

Protect every one of them.

"John, I… don't…."

"Just breathe. It's okay, Love. I'm with you. Just breathe."

Maples Cold November Leaves Rakes Pumpkins Icy Past Halloween My Birth

On That Day

Saints Rosaries

Tree Gravity Handprints Leaning

Night Comes

Chill

Soft Roots

Chill

Looking Up

Chill

Safe World

Slowing

           slowing

                    slowing

                              slowing

down

down

chill

down

landing

Trunk

Leaning

I don't think there is a verb in the English language that describes that moment. The silence became a scream. I started weeping and sobbing and choking and singing and landing as John's voice pulled me back to my skin and my shoes with rag wool socks and my weird obsession with old man cardigan sweaters and wondering why corduroy pants aren't popular anymore and John's voice resonating into a tone.

"Brian, I'll fly there right now. I don't know what's going on, but I'll fly there if you need me. I'll fly there right now."

You're here now. I feel you.

The blood flowed back the right direction, and my eyes focused on the tree trunk that anchored me. My planet had returned to my orbit, and I could feel the edges of my fingers again, and my vision could now see the bark on the tree.

I couldn't understand what he was saying, so I pushed words forward to make him feel safe.

I said, "I'm okay. I'll call when I'm back to the hotel."

John replied, "Brian, you're coming home early. You know these long trips away don't work. I miss you and besides, I made homemade pizza last weekend. It didn't taste as good as it normally does. You make everything better."

Is he lying? That can't be true. I'm too broken for you.

John said, "I love you. Lily and Nash love you too. We all can't wait to get you home."

"Love you too." Lily's sweet eyes that called to me from across glass at a humane society. Nash's frozen eyes from a puppy mill finding his voice and not pooping blood any longer. No streams of blood on the pavement when I walked him. Nash was walking and I was walking. He was showing me, and I was showing him the beauty of this world.

The phone went quiet, and I placed it in my pocket as I wiped the sludge of snot from my nose and mouth. I realized that I vomited. Why does every big moment for me involve vomit?

There was a rainbow bright pile of vomit with dark red pieces swimming about, and I could hear John saying, "If you eat too many sweets, you'll get sick to your stomach."

Then, I felt her tap. I turned around instinctively, and I immediately wished that I could undo the automatic response to any human being tapped by another human.

There she stood – Lois!

"Harold, it's the tapper. That's the tapper from the movie," Lois said as she looked me up and down to size up the Great Tapper. As she observed what a wreck I was, she said, "Are you okay?"

Her husband said, "Lois, I'm the tapper. Remember?"

Lois smiled broadly showing all her teeth, saying, "I know, Harold. I'm teasing."

I said what I had learned to say for over thirty years since the nights of darkness and memories fading, "I'm okay. I just had something upset my stomach."

Harold now came over and stood with Lois carrying a brown paper bag in his hand and the only coffee cup New Yorkers seemed to use, the blue one with Greek lettering that I only knew Starbucks didn't offer.

Lois said, "You know, Love. You're clearly far from home, and I'm a mother. Don't lie to a mother." She then grabbed the paper bag from Harold who immediately looked like a forlorn child. She then reached into the bag and grabbed out a stacked pastry with a squiggly line of chocolate frosting across the top. She said, "Have you ever had a Napoleon? You've never really been to New York if you haven't had a Napoleon."

I was shocked if I'm honest. How had our relationship as fierce enemies standing on the border of our conflict ended up with pastry being shoved in my teary-eyed face? Lois moved forward and said in a mother's voice no living person can ignore, saying, "Go on! Take it!"

I obliged, holding this creamy dessert in both hands.

Harold then said, "This stranger doesn't need both of them."

Lois replied, "For God's sake Harold, I only gave him one."

She then touched my shoulder, and she smiled at me. It felt like the longest ten seconds of my life, but I knew she could see.

She said, "Honey, I'm sorry someone hurt you. I really am, Love. Will you do something for me that my mother told me to do? She told me one day when I was sure my world had ended to laugh. She told me that laughing at our demons makes them recoil. I dare you to try it."

I replied, staring at this gigantic pastry looking ready to fall apart in my hands, saying, "That's sound advice. Thanks Lois."

Harold shrugged and handed me a napkin from the bag. I tried to thank him, but he said, "She's right on this one." Then, he reached into the bag and began shoving the pastry into his mouth.

Lois then looked back at Harold and grinned and she said as sarcastically as possible, "He's my Superman, you get me? He's going to rescue me at some point."

"It's true. I'd rescue you anytime you needed me, but I have a feeling she'd be rescuing me," Harold replied. They both laughed, and I had no choice but to join them.

Lois said, "The real Superman is an old Jewish lady from Brooklyn. Why not?" We laughed as the demons of the moment that brought me to my knees faded into the past.

Lois continued, "My mother said, 'Don't let an asshole ruin your life. They aren't worth it. You hear me?"

Harold nodded as his wife dropped Zen-monk level wisdom on my ass.

Lois said, "You hearin' me, Love?"

I said for the first time in my life in a way that even I believed it, "Yes."

As I made my way to the Subway station, I had yellow pudding all over my front shirt, vomit on my shoes, and rivers of crusted snot and tears that made it look like the Hindenburg exploded in my sinus cavity. I looked and felt like a failed methadone clinic.

I took a finger down the front shirt with enough yellow pudding to satisfy my final bite, and I licked them clean. I was the crazy nutjob on the subway that day and I was grateful for the new life awaiting me as each stop whisked by.

Chapter 10

THE TALE OF TWO COWS AND A GURU

Through the digital world of Zoomlandia many of us inhabited during the pandemic, a student once asked me from her glowing square, "Brian, what's the number one thing a developing medium can do to grow in their link?"

I thought about this for a moment. I hate 'What's the one thing?' questions. It always feels like the TOP FIVE WAYS TO GET THE HOT GUY TO MAKEOUT WITH YOU articles (By the way, if you're wondering, watermelon lip gloss! It has never failed me. Just saying…), but I'm on the spot. I'm supposed to be smart about this whole thing, so I put on my spiritual hat where deep thoughts flow from a holy fountain of wisdom. I was in the 'GURU ZONE.'

All joking aside, for me, the answer is always gratitude. People hate how simple this is, but it's absolutely the truth.

When the miracle of this work isn't enough for a person, they are in a battle with their egos many won't win. I will never forget when I personally learned this lesson of gratitude. It changed everything.

#

When I was doing my initial training in Reiki, my instructor kept mentioning meditation as if all of us knew what the heck she was saying. I looked around and saw the other four participants in my course nod appropriately. I finally got the courage to raise my hand and ask, "How do you meditate? I suck at meditation. I want that peace and focus, but I'm the worst meditator in the world."

She laughed with me and smiled in her peaceful way. "Brian, meditation is as private as a prayer. Only you can learn how to meditate. Many people will make up many rules, but meditation is all about connecting to the light."

The light? What light? Maybe only smart people who do yoga regularly can connect with the light.

My instructor then said a magical thing that forever changed my door to meditation: "My cat taught me how to meditate. She and I would stare at one another, and I would try to match her softness and her gentle presence with my breath. I used her eyes at first but then I could simply feel if we were aligned."

My yoga teacher is that crazy person making cat videos. I'm certain of it!

I asked, "Yes, but how do you get started?"

She paused. I imagined her initiating a quiet, connected space by bathing herself in blessed water from a sacred monastery in Botswana, then dancing nude while sage-ing herself. She said, "I think of one person or animal that loves me for who I am, and I imagine them holding my hand."

WTF? Can it really be that easy?

I nodded as I had learned to do in multiple math classes since kindergarten—I had no clue what she had just said.

Now, I was on a mission to learn to meditate. I would be the best meditator in the world. I would even try out for an Olympic team of meditators. I would become the Dalai Brian. Too much? Yup.

Because I was driving a long way from our little cabin in the woods to Denver every day, I had ample time to consider how to meditate better. It was time to learn what meditation was all about. As I was driving, I'd turn down my music and center myself. I'd imagine being held in the arms of a surrogate grandmother in my childhood neighborhood. I could see her eyes and her smile as she greeted me every day. I would keep doing my breathing as the light of Spirit began to....

"NICE driving, Asshat!" I yelled, shaking my raised fist at the white Ford F-250 truck that had just passed me and almost forced my car into a ditch. I meditated on all the ways I could make that blockhead realize he was a complete jerk. On his bumper, he had stickers with large-breasted women blowing kisses from cherry red lips. Another sticker sparkled with the silvery words "God Bless You!" Two silver balls dangled from the rear chassis, and they swished side to side with every swerve. Freud wouldn't have been able to make sense of the multiple competing images. I felt badly for his future therapist. Then, I centered and searched my newly meditated heart for the place of inner beauty where the dancing lights of spirit would embrace me in the fire of my truth. (Clearly, I needed help, and it would take a very special teacher.)

Long ago, I decided I was the unofficial hall monitor of all highways, and let's just say I'm kind of amazing at it. No one offered me the position. Let's just say some folks just find a way to be of living service. I'm super evolved that way. Not everyone would know the perfectly mature way to respond to a driver acting like a jerk on the road, but my Catholic education obviously prepared me for it. Asshat!

After the white truck was well out of sight and I'd calmed myself, I continued my profound meditation journey by taking a breath and returning to my meditative space ... until, that is, the slowest Honda Civic in the world (with several "Save the Whales" stickers gleaming on its bumper) wound its way lazily down the road in front of me. Really? One annoying driver wasn't enough? "Hurry up, Grandma Jean!" I decided to pass her on the only straightaway on Blue Creek Road. I raised my middle finger politely, screaming "Kale-Loving Commie" as I screeched by. (I get it. I basically just described myself. If I add a "Miss," "Kale-Loving Commie" could be my perfect drag persona.) I told you, I'm good at this. Some might say amazing.

Instead of giving Grandma the finger, I took a breath and returned to the soft place where only love, light, and peace and hope exist for all eternity.

Okay! I admit it. I suck at meditation. The Dalai Lama would have even given up on me. But over the coming weeks, I'd learn patience and virtue from the strangest of mentors - Bessie. She had her work cut out for her.

Week 1

The following day, as I drove up the Blue Creek Road, I decided to enjoy a detour along a four-mile, two-lane road that goes through beautiful pastoral farm country and leads to Brook Forest Road and then home. As I was driving, I noticed a field to my right, with roughly nine Holstein cows. Holsteins are the largest dairy-producing cows and are well-known for their unique markings. Their white bodies with odd black spots make them look like they've been painted by a graffiti artist. I decided to pull over and watch them for a while.

Seven of the cows rested in a small group under a tree, two were off and away from the group, grazing in a meadow. As I approached the split rail fence, the group of cows froze. Then, one large cow (whom I named Bessie) walked away from the tree and stared at me. She looked pissed. The other six cows moved away from the tree and walked into the meadow. Bessie remained fixed in her spot. She stared at me. I stared back. After a while, I began to soften my breath. I would find peace and focus if it killed me. Ten minutes passed. The other cows were grazing comfortably, but Bessie did not change in any way.

Holsteins have such unique coloring. I placed my hand on my heart, focused on the unique black stains on their bodies, and imagined what shapes I could see. One cow's markings looked like a clown, his lips pursed, blowing bubbles. Another's looked like dotted islands in the

South Pacific, spreading out into an archipelago. Another's looked like a train car, sputtering smoke from her rear flank all the way to her eyes. The images seemed to shift and change, the same way clouds expand and dissipate. I softened my gaze. I tried to decide, am I daydreaming or meditating? Unsure, I realized I was giving myself a Rorschach Test. Psychiatrists would certainly have found my interpretations diagnostically interesting.

I realized: I've got to pee. Normally, any little bush along a country road would do, but I could feel Bessie's eyes boring into me. How would Heisenberg feel about this moment? I climbed into my car and sped away, with a full bladder and a swollen mind.

I visited Bessie every day that week. The ritual seemed to repeat itself every day. I knew who my teacher was. Bessie's eyes greeted me with disdain each time. She stood her ground; the other cows moved away. I thought about holding grass for her in my hands, but that felt like cheating. Instead, I stood by the fence and continued to soften my presence through my breath and through focusing on gratitude.

On the fifth day, even though Bessie did not shift an inch, I noticed a change in me. I was softer with John when I got home. I went to bed earlier. The following week, I decided to stop again to see what might happen.

Week 2

On Monday, Bessie took her defensive position instantly. I took my position too, resting my right leg on the fence. I felt more relaxed. I noticed that each of the cows had a different personality. I never named them because Bessie alone was my focus. However, I started to see small things. One of the cows took longer to stand than the others. She walked slower than her group, seeming to wince on her back leg. Another cow seemed smaller than the rest. She barely looked at me, she was focused on her never-ending salad bar. The other cows were ignoring me more and more. I began to see them all as separate. What had been just a field of cows became a diverse group with different markings, different challenges. For three days in the second week, Bessie didn't move an inch. Her sideways profile with her big brown eyes let me know that she was the real fence, and I was an intruder.

The same scenario occurred every day: me and Bessie locked in a staring contest. Then, on Thursday, I tried something different. I softened my breath, and I began to feel gratitude for her. I noticed her. I saw the weathered skin on her legs, her small hooves. It makes no sense how those skinny legs can sustain the weight of a mature female cow all day long, in the heat. It is astonishing and beautiful. Even graceful.

On Friday, a miracle happened. I began as I always had I softened my breath. Bessie took her place on her same spot. But the others never moved from their place near the tree. Bessie's eyes seem to have softened somehow. She seemed curious about me in the same way I was curious about her. I felt sincere love for her. I said softly, "I love you, Bessie. I love you." I moved my eyes up and down her body, and for the first time I noticed where she had been branded. The borders of the brand showed a large D and L. The upper loop on the L was burned deeply into her skin. The skin looked melted; no fur grew there. Insects congregated on the edge of the fur and skin. Her tail could not hit that spot or provide any relief from that nuisance and pain. It looked like an old burn. I had a flash image of the moment she was branded; the searing heat spreading across her body, Bessie screaming, trying to catch her breath.

How could I not have noticed that brand? Two weeks had passed! In that moment, I was ashamed. I hadn't really seen Bessie at all. I had been so focused on my outcome—her coming to the fence to greet me—that I didn't see how the afternoon wind lifted her beautiful black hair, how that made her look softer, even more beautiful. I whispered that I loved her and told her how sorry I was for the pain she had experienced. Bessie. Her name had shape. She was a personality, with eyes of dark moonlight.

I kept imagining some farmer with a shotgun coming by, telling me to stop harassing the cows. My response would have been, "I'm not cow-tipping. I'm just hanging with Bessie." That would certainly have resulted in a seventy-two-hour hold, but this was as real an interaction as I have ever had with a human being. I knew my time with Bessie was complete for that day, and my pups needed me at home. "Thank you, Bessie," I said. She responded by doing something she had never done before—she walked away and began to graze, no longer standing watch. The fence had disappeared.

I know that this was not the outcome you might have imagined: Bessie coming to me, me embracing her across the fence. But I will never forget that moment. By no longer guarding her group, Bessie had said everything. At that moment, even though I don't remember ever placing it there, I noticed that my right hand was placed over my heart. I thanked Bessie, got in my car, and drove away. I couldn't wait to visit her on Monday to see what new experience awaited us.

I drove up Blue Creek Road on the next Monday afternoon. No cows. I was heartbroken. I stood by the fence and imagined where they might have gone. When I got home, I told John. He replied, "Brian, in late fall, they move livestock to lower elevations for the winter. They do this every season."

His answer made sense, but still, what would I do without Bessie? How could I meditate on higher beings and become ascended without her? Damn it! (Yes, I know, I've got work to do.) Bessie taught me so many things. She left me with a softer place inside me, and to this day, I picture Bessie in that field, teaching me to see with new eyes. Who said a strong and powerful Holstein can't be an angel? Although, she did prove Miss Hot Yoga Pants McGee right. Maybe this was Bessie's final gift. I'm a reluctant student, but Bessie was the perfect guru. I had no idea that her lessons were just beginning.

#

"Brian," Kim said, "I have breast cancer. I'm scared." Then, the other side of the phone was filled with breathless whimpers and heaving cries that come from that low place in the gut where fear and sadness meet.

Oh no! This can't be happening. Kim has breast cancer. In less than five seconds, everything in my world was changing. My dearest friend and sister from a different mister was dealing with the ugly, horrifying "C" word.

After I caught my breath, she told me everything she had been told. I listened. The game of musical chairs was on. Would Kim take the final seat when the music stopped? Would cancer claim it? Her mother and her father had played the game and lost. After their surgery, radiation, and chemotherapy, their chairs were empty. Her mother was taken first, her father many years later.

As I hung up the phone, I looked at the calendar on my phone. Less than four month ago, my mom had died. Today, my best friend was fighting for her life. In that tempest of worry, I remembered a powerful moment I had spent with Kim with the sea cow, Margie (or as she is formally known, Margie the Manatee). It was the second time a cow had changed my path, both in meditation and in life.

Kim had come up with this crazy idea for us to take a couple of hours on our way to an educational conference in Florida to swim with the manatees. It had been a dream of hers, and I was happy to oblige.

It was mid-February and cold outside. After signing up for a half-day tour with a smaller group, we were on the dock awaiting the captain's directions for selecting the properly-sized snorkel, mask, and wetsuit. Every time he grinned, the captain's sun-soaked smile made it look as if he was tightening a sheet across his cheeks, and his low-timbered voice (from many years of ignoring warning labels on cigarette packs) made him feel like a distant friend or relative. "You'll need a large, Chief!" he told me.

I put down the medium wetsuit I was holding and grabbed an already-wet suit with an L written on it in black marker. I imagined the previous wearer's nickname: Tiny. I doubted that the suits had been professionally cleaned, and as I felt the wetsuit dangle against my legs, I hoped the previous person really liked soap. There was no way to Purell myself through this one.

As the large houseboat moved away from the shore, I watched as our group of eight struggled to stretch and pull on the wetsuits assigned to us. Mine was a black, faded suit with a yellow lightning bolt, and it required every known muscle in my body to pull the wet fabric up over my body. It reminded me of my horrible high school physics professor repeating over and over again about the friction coefficient and its influence over any object traveling in the x-direction. As I ripped, pulled, and stretched the black suit over folds of skin, in that cold, wet, uncomfortable moment, I realized that my over-forty friction coefficient was significant.

I looked to my right. Miss Kim Ortiz sat comfortably, staring out the window enjoying the scenery. Her wetsuit was pulled perfectly up to her chest. As the last bit of fabric rested comfortably against her chest, she was clearly unaware of a friction coefficient. This was Kim in a nutshell. She was almost oblivious to the major struggles of my life, because the tune she heard in her ears was one of wonder and joy. Even with her advanced degrees in mathematics and her bizarre habit of doing calculus story problems for relaxation, she had this soft place where she lived. We were in the same spot in completely different worlds, and I was simply grateful she was willing to be in my orbit.

I stared at her. The brown highlights in her long black hair reflected sunlight, her brown eyes gazed into the distance. She was excited, focused on the moment she had dreamed of for many years. This small houseboat (from hell) had the loudest trolling motor in the world. It moved through the river with the stealth of a Hells Angels motorcycle gang.

"Now, you can take pictures, you can take your memories, but you can't take the manatees home with you," Captain Jack announced. It was clear he had repeated this line one too many times; he delivered it dead-pan and humorlessly. "There are volunteers on kayaks, there to ensure you do not harass the manatees. The manatees must approach you. Does everyone understand this?" The rest of his speech covered the details, a fine for breaking the rules, etc. Then he handed out masks and snorkels to each person.

As the captain turned off the boat's engine and the sliding glass door of this rectangular behemoth came to a stop, we could hear the symphony of sounds from the Crystal River sanctuary. The birds in the trees sang melodies back and forth as our boat moved up and down in the quiet water. The gentle waves made me think of that familiar image of a woman sitting in the moon, dangling her feet off the moon as if it were a hammock. Her toes moved back and forth gently as our boat rose and fell. She was calm today, so the waves were too.

As we lowered our bodies into the Crystal River, the mid-February chill of the water took my breath away, but Kim was smiling from ear-to-ear. She moved through the river confidently and the OMG Holy Crap chill-you-to-the-bone water seemed to only increase her resolve. As we moved farther, we could see that the area where the manatees hung out had a bright yellow rope spread across it. We had been told not to enter that space. As we moved closer, the eight other tourists on the boat were grappling with their cameras and yelling to one another.

I caught up to Kim and whispered to her, "Follow me. I have an idea." I moved in the opposite direction, and we placed ourselves on the opposite side to where the group was standing. As we stood there in water up to our chests, we held hands and moved around to stay warm.

"Brian, I have an idea. Think of something you're grateful for."

"Why? I'm freezing my ass off!"

"Then, be grateful you have an ass."

In earnest, we both closed our eyes and thought of something. Instantly, my little pup Lily appeared in my mind. My twenty-three-pound beagle mix, Lily, loves me in a way that has changed me. I imagined holding her in my arms in that moment and felt instantly grateful.

We opened our eyes—a humongous female manatee was coming near us. Her baby was directly next to her. She circled us for a while, then she went through my legs and wrapped her flippers around my legs. I was in shock. She was lying in the water, her head facing up, staring at me with such gentleness and kindness. Her baby swam around me and then began kissing my face. As I rubbed the mama manatee on the chest, she stared at me. She was so beautiful. I felt the many scars on her body from propellers on boats that had sped through these waters. I couldn't even feel angry about this; it was obvious that she wasn't. I used one hand to pet the baby on his whiskers while my other hand made large circles on the mama's chest. The mother moved through my legs, went to Kim, and attached herself to her in the exact same way.

When the rest of our group saw what was happening, they came over to take pictures and to make their own connection. But the large group was clearly too much for the mama manatee, and she and her baby crossed the sacred rope and disappeared into the aggregation of manatees.

We went back to the boat to warm up for a while, and then decided to go back one more time. I remembered to be in that energy of gratitude, and I held the image of my Miss Lily again. As we approached the exact same spot, the mama manatee came to join us. We had more time with her and the baby was even more animated. But once again, the large, selfie-hungry tourists rushed over, juggling their cameras and screaming. The mama and baby swam away. I decided to head back to the boat to commiserate with Kim about how awful tourists are.

As I headed back, Kim called out, "Are you cold, honey? Drink hot coffee, I'll be right there to help get you warm."

I replied, "The manatees left."

Kim replied, "They'll be back, I want to ensure other folks have the same experience."

The captain greeted me by saying, "Welcome back, Chief! I saw you out there with Margie! Isn't she amazing?"

I replied appropriately as his un-filtered Camel cigarette grew a line of ash that seemed to defy gravity.

I sat on the bench and peeled off the wetsuit. I glanced over at Kim in the water. Margie and her baby circled her as tourists took turns touching the manatees and getting their pictures taken. Kim stood, smiling from ear-to-ear as the tourists moved closer to her and the manatees. I felt so inspired by her. She has always been a mentor for me in all things. She is an example of how courageous I hope to be one day. She is the slow driver who makes the world a safer place; she has always had eyes that see beyond herself.

Kim has that presence of peace and hopefulness that seems to attract everyone to her, and I had my full circle moment. Kim was showing me how the world looks through her beautiful brown eyes when you have both of these attributes in place for a long, long time. For Kim, every soul is another chance to practice love and every moment is another chance to remind others that they matter. For Kim, every moment is a meditative moment, a time to tap into kindness and gratitude.

Kim isn't battling cancer; she is embracing it. She is letting the lesson hold her in the water. She is trusting the experience, even as she grieves the new body and the different life on the other side of this experience. She softens in the face of adversity. As I place my hand on my heart, I know I am part of her, and she will forever be a part of me. Kim is the best meditator in the world and should be called the Kimmy Lama.

Of course, back then, I made the goals of meditation about me. But now I realize that that space of meditation and surrender is actually the opposite. Meditation allows me to see you. It is a reminder to me that we only have this moment. I don't want to waste it being enamored with my pain. My pain connects me to you, because neither you nor I can do this journey alone. Our life journeys connect us to one another and my pursuit of becoming the best meditator in the world led me to you. This was the seed for the life I have today and for me, and it is one of the foundations of mediumship.

So, recall that at the beginning of this chapter, we were in my Reiki meditation class and I was trying to grasp the essentials and techniques of meditation. That led me to Bessie, my first true meditation mentor. I just know that one day in the distant future, I will be driving down that same country road. Maybe, I'll see "Grandma Jean" again ... the slow driver with her Save the Whales bumper sticker. This time, I'll imagine her bumper sticker reads Save the Cows Too!

Chapter 11

THE DAY THE GOLDEN GIRLS MET WHINY BUTT MCGEE

I was driving home after a long day. This was the time when I was working full-time during the day in a school district and at night, I was becoming a family therapist doing my internship every evening. I was sustaining myself with a Taco Bell Supreme Burrito and Sour Skittles.

All of the sudden, this crazy nut job with a store-bought perm kit, that must have been on sale or the bitch got robbed, pulled out in front of me in her sunflower yellow VW Beetle on Leetsdale Avenue heading towards Monaco Parkway at roughly 9:27 PM. She almost hit me as she switched lanes in front of me, and my burrito supreme spilled out of its fragile shell leaving me covered in the not so supreme contents. As my life flashed before my eyes, my first thought was, they didn't put any sour cream on this! If I had died, that would have been my last thought.

I then watched as her vehicle never made it fully into the far-right lane of the three. I imagined the drinks she'd been having and the party she'd attended. Then, I saw her bumper sticker:

I WISH I WAS THE PERSON MY DOG THINKS I AM

I rolled down my window and politely yelled, "Crazy Ass Perm Pam, you're not! You're a crazy bitch!"

I hate getting guidance from shitty drivers with bad perms, but somehow, it's often those I disregard quickly who teach me things I didn't know I needed. I normally hate any messages that insist I aim for a goal mere mortals can never attain.

I WISH I WAS THE PERSON MY DOG THINKS I AM.

I could still hear my sponsor say on the phone with his perfectly tuned to a monk vibe voice, saying, "Now Brian, are you sure you don't have an anger problem?"

Me? Little ole' me?

I caught my breath after screaming at some poor soul. That bumper sticker haunted me, and I kept wondering how I could become the person my dog thinks I am.

Dogs forgive.

They do. They know how to forgive.

They don't put the entire history of the way the world has harmed them on every other future person they meet. Every person is given the chance to connect.

Some might think they forget. If you've ever been with a traumatized dog, you know that is not the case.

But they do forgive.

I still had my list, and I was checking it twice. I still had fantasies of God making people who had been jerks to me in life being forced to stay in after-death detention and having to watch on repeat all the ways in which they had hurt me, even though I had only ever been lovely in every way.

The memory of being in Scott Jackman's basement, who was my sponsor in a twelve-step program, all came flooding back to me.

I remember the courageous and rigorous inventory Scott invited me to do (Did I say invited? Ha!!!!). I had always been and still am if I'm honest The Hall Monitor for the Universe, even though no one had ever asked me. I happily took on that task and wore my sash under my clothes my entire life, insisting to myself that if people would just get their shit together, I would be fine.

Well, that's what I thought I was doing anyway.

Alanon is the sister twelve-step group where we learn how to accept that we are, indeed, perfect and lovely, even as alcoholics and addicts and other pains in the ass we attract into our path are always the real problem.

Not us, mind you. We're lovely.

NOT!

You can tell from this paragraph that the work doesn't always work.

That day, an alcoholic named Scott who became my sponsor through no fault of his own, taught me about what happens when mirrors speak back to the past.

I brought my long list of people who had failed me, and I was ready for the pity party he had promised. Finally, someone would honor how terrible some of these folks were on my list. As I begin my process of explaining to Scott why my life has been far more challenging than anyone else, he kept pausing and saying, "What price do you pay for not giving him grace?" Or "Oh! I'm sorry. I thought we were working on you today. No, please keep whining."

By lunch, Scott likely wanted to go out and drink after thirty years of sobriety, but he lived in the suburbs of Omaha, Nebraska with three other even older sober gay men I called "The Golden Girls."

Dorothy, the Irish and still very Catholic Bostonian in his sixties who came out after his wife died of cancer, yells down the stairs, "How's he doing down there? Is he starting to see he's the one that is the problem?" His Irish mobster look with his cardigan sweater and the perpetual smell of Vicks fills my nostrils as he hugs me close.

Scott says with his hands raised as if he's coaching a losing team, "These Alanons love their pain. They are addicted to their pain. Alcoholics drink because of Alanons. I swear to God!"

The Golden Girls guffawed and pulled out a chair at the kitchen table after we emerged from my pit of despair. This table had become home for this wayward gay soul, and I felt home in a way I seldom had in the past three years.

The cook of the family - Blanche, had her full-body frilly apron on and little else. He dyed the few hairs he had left on his head and his chest hair. It was clearly a Just for Men fail, but no one was going to ever tell him. He looked right at me and smiled from ear to ear. "Come and give me some sugar!" as he embraced me and kissed me right on my forehead. He continued, "Do you like your chili the way you like your men? Spicy?" I smiled from ear to ear.

I was learning if someone teases you, this is another form of love.

Then, to round out our triad, Rose rounded them out at our table of five. Rose leaned over and said, "Now Brian, don't let those old queens get you so angry. They mean well. After all, we were gay long before you knew the sky was blue. Among us, we have one hundred years of sobriety and almost that many years of being gay. I don't know how Alanons measure their growth, but you still get chips, right?"

Scott chimed in, "Brian is getting his one year at the Bellevue meeting next week. They have him doing a five-minute share. He says he's an alcoholic still, but we discuss all the time that's likely going to need to change. He's nuts, but he doesn't drink."

Dorothy, with his thick Bostonian accent, chimes in, saying, "Now Brian, those Bellevue people expect ties and nice slacks. They don't fuck around, and you have to lower the volume on the gay thing there.

It's what I call Conservative Christian kind of like church AA, but their sobriety is sobriety. Lots of lives have been saved in their meetings."

I ask, "I didn't know Bellevue had extremist nut jobs! Why the hell do people like us need to go there? I spent my whole life trying to escape places like that."

Rose said, "My first sponsor was from Bellevue, and I cherish every word he said to me that got me here. They are us and we are them. Look for what is similar. We're all trying to quiet the fire before it burns us. Don't you know that by now?"

I reply, "I'm sorry but I cannot agree. I'm not going to a place where they don't want me. I'm sick of always bending myself into different shapes to fit through doors others create for me and others like me. I'm so sick of it!"

As Blanche brings over the chili, he spoons out big heaping portions of chili and he looks right at me, saying, "Honey, if you spend your whole life being angry that this world doesn't accept you as God made you, then you'll always be limited by the joy their ignorance allows. What a stupid way to live! Would you not throw out a life raft to someone who is drowning, or would you interview them first to ensure they were worth your time?"

I was so sick of this Pollyanna crap that made me feel guilty for the way the world had failed me. I tried one last time to get them to see how much I'd been hurt by those with privilege. I had one last Hail Mary so they could see the scars of my experience, hoping this time, they would hear.

I said, "I've been beaten down for too long and suffered too many indignities at the hands of so-called Christians. Of course, they believe in confession. They are ignorant bullies to any group of people they deem to be less than them and they use their ancient text written by prehistoric bullies to justify their cruelty and chosen ignorance. I'm done being the nice guy. You really think I'm going to celebrate a year of my recovery by standing in front of the very people with different names but the same damn haircuts to thank God for the new life I have. You really think I'm going to bow down and wear a fucking tie to obey their church-like rituals so I can..."

"Stop! Just stop!," Scott yelled and we all quieted as Blanche slurped up his chili as an episode of The Gays of Our Lives was seemingly playing on his TV and I was the lead actor.

Scott paused and looked at me, "Do you honestly think I give a fuck what any of those people think of you, me, or any other person from our community? I am not seeking their approval. I'm having you stand up and get your chip so the gay man in that room just like me who is hiding from who he is for many years and hating himself. We go into those spaces so they can't say they don't know a gay person, and we go to show being who we are is simply honoring who God made us to be. Can't you see that?"

Rose chimed in, adding as he grabbed my hands, "There will be one, maybe even two, and who the hell knows? Possibly even three people in that audience of over one hundred people who will see you celebrating your life. And who knows? Maybe, just maybe, some of the ignorant homophobes will think differently about how they treat their son or daughter that sits them down one day and says, "Mom, I think I'm gay."

Scott was crying at this point, and I felt all the wind of my purpose dissipate. The table became completely silent as Scott's feelings of the past rose and made us all freeze.

Blanche then said, "What if your words that are spoken from your heart plant a seed of a different possibility for that kid on that day in that living room? You don't want to be part of that? It's a fucking privilege to be a part of that."

I looked around to see if anyone would soften the blows of the truth bombs dropped on that table. I was shaken like a tree after a storm, and I was left trying to decide which leaves needed to be released and which ones would become even more sacred.

I looked at Scott and waited for his eyes to join mine. He had taught me this very technique half a million times, and I said, "I am so embarrassed. I thought getting the chip was for me. I can see now…"

Scott interrupted me, saying, "Brian, why do we have to choose? Can't both purposes exist in the same space? Is there a greater way to show you are grateful that you're not dead in a bathtub than to offer your moment of success to others who are staring down the razor you escaped by the tiniest hairs on your chin? Have you still not learned that gratitude is an action that makes everything else work?"

That night, I wore the tie Scott gave me. I tucked in my white button-up shirt and Scott held that token in his hand as he shared how much he loved me that night. I knew the love he offered me that year was a force I could not match. I knew there would be a day when I would need to become that Love, but I couldn't even imagine it.

It was a couple months later when a man came to the Friday Night Super Gay All the Time Twelve-Step Meeting and said, "My name is Michael, and I'm an alcoholic. I didn't know you all were here, but my sponsor told me that someone spoke at our weekly Bellevue meeting. I've held a secret for a long time.... and..... it almost.... killed me." The sentence finally found its period, and then this six-foot-tall man with wavy brown hair collapsed on the table and sobbed.

I tried not to look at Miss Jackman because I was sure her penetrating stare was searing a hole in my head. I could just imagine the "Told Ya So" expression coming back my way and I'd seen so many of those looks when I strayed off the path in the past year. I finally looked over at him as we all stood for the Lord's Prayer where I changed it to "Our Mother" at the beginning just because that's how I roll.

When I looked at him, Scott was wiping his tears as he looked at me.

He made a circle with his hand on his heart and mouthed the words "I love you."

Then, I'm sure that old queen turned on her heels and said, "Told you so."

You certainly did, Scott.

Scott said as we left that meeting that night, "You're now a sponsor, Brian. Don't fuck it up!"

I asked, "How will I know what to do?"

He looked at me and then held my hands in his, saying, "Honey, now that you know your backpack isn't heavier than any other soul at these tables, you have a responsibility to love everyone else into trusting their own backpack of lessons. When someone honors you by sharing their pain, you will begin to see the face of God in every person."

Chapter 12

THE THRONE OF A BETTER QUEEN

I remember the jars they had lined up on a table showing the development of a fetus. The table placard said THE MIRACLE OF LIFE.

The obvious intention of this was to show us how a human life develops over time. We were meant to feel a sense of protection for the innocent baby being offered by the hands of God to this world.

The instructor said, "Can you believe a baby looks so perfect and complete so early in the journey of pregnancy? This beautiful life is waiting for you to embrace it."

Attending an all-boys Catholic school, this was part of our Sex Ed discussion. The other three days were pictures of every horrible STD one could get if they chose sex before marriage. Even for a gay kid, it was confusing. Was it that life is beautiful or that sex is evil?

Then, they showed us the video of an abortion in a late term situation. The graphic and violent content made any person with a beating heart want to scream out to rescue the innocent child this horrible doctor was murdering.

I looked around and the common reaction was tears and incredulity of what forces of humanity could possibly stand in opposition to a life. How dare they be so selfish?? (Whoever 'they' was)

All pumped up and primed to fight for babies who were being innocently ripped from wombs of terrible mothers, I sat down on my mother's bed and told her what had occurred at school. I was ready for us to join the army of souls against abortion!!

I've found that, as a gay son, my mother's bedroom always felt like an altar. When I wasn't trying on her nylons in the closet or trying to walk in her heels in the basement, I was happy to simply observe her. I now see why homophobia and sexism are the same fight on the same battlefield.

I needed to see my mother on her throne to share my new zealotry. I think I wanted her validation and her blessing in my new crusade.

"Mom, I learned about saving babies today."

I wondered if she'd heard me. She looked towards the window and smoked her cigarette, releasing billows of smoke from the lowest quadrant of her lungs making a rasping sound as she retrieved oxygen from the air. She was never going to let a little thing like asthma keep her from enjoying her two-pack a day habit. So, I did what I'm best at. I kept talking and talking as the major highlights of the week seemed to rise like smoke rings above her before she could honor the profound wisdom of her desperately trying to be a good Catholic gay boy.

She listened intently and, after my prolonged speech detailing the horrors from the video, she said, "Brian, what did they teach you about the mother?"

I was caught off guard and I was irritated she asked me a distracting question like this. After all, she's Catholic too. Did I need to get that video and a priest to help me ensure she saw the light?

Maybe, she needed an exorcism!!

"No," I replied. "That's not really the point. It's killing babies! This isn't complicated."

"My good friend called me one night many years ago and told me she was finally ready to leave her abusive husband. Then, she cried into the phone, letting me know she was pregnant. She told me she was broken and didn't know what to do. She asked for my guidance. Brian, you seem so certain of these matters after a week of videos. So, what should I have told her?"

I replied, "Your friend had an abortion? I don't believe you. You wouldn't know someone like that."

My mother continued, saying, "Isn't that interesting? You made some huge assumptions there. I'm just asking. What should I have told my friend?"

I replied, "I don't know. Tell her, "Life is sacred!""

My mother replied, "Is her life sacred?"

I said, "I don't know. You're trying to trick me."

My mother had a long dangling log of cigarette waiting to fall at any minute and make another lava hole in her comforter. She ignored this hazard and kept staring right at me.

My mother then said, "That's exactly right. You don't know. You have no clue what that moment meant to her or to me."

I asked, "Well, did she? Did she get the abortion?"

My mother looked even more frustrated with me and she looked around her bedroom for some imaginary person to step in and take over this lecture.

My mother said, "Brian, that's none of your business. Is she the hero if she kept the baby or the enemy if she made a different choice?"

I replied confidently, "I know what I'd do! It's not confusing for me."

My mom said, "Do you? I'm grateful it's easy for you. Then, what should I have told her?"

I whispered, "I hope she kept the baby."

My mom said, "That's her business. You'll likely be faced with a moment when a girl you love reaches out to let you know she's pregnant and the baby is yours. From that moment that baby arrives, your world will never be the same. What you don't understand is that the woman carrying your baby has forever died to the person she once was. Her world has already changed her identity and the world will demand she's happy about it."

I reflected on this, and I was starting to see how crazy it all seemed. At that age, it felt as if my brain was contracting past the boxes my mind had created. I said, "That doesn't seem fair. I hadn't even considered how big of a deal this is. I really don't know what she should do."

I saw tears rise in her eyes and she said, "Just remember that you don't know. That's the most loving thing a man can say. If you ever imagine you do, then you'll be dangerous to any woman who loves you."

Let's just say no woman has ever made that call. I can't imagine why.

As I reflect, I can recognize there were chains on my mother's soul I refused to honor. There's nothing more painful than denying someone's reality. I can never be more than I was with her, but I can hopefully become that with my dear friends.

However, I am blessed for the ways her wisdom arrived on the side of her bed doing her best to reclaim the parts of her our Catholic world dishonored. I'm grateful to remember just how courageous it was for her to stand against the tides that tried to rip me from her dignity into a land of certainty. It was never wisdom my school offered that week about abortion. It was a simple story that tried to silence the complex one. They told me simple tales of morality but the women I love have never walked in that world. It would be nothing less than cruel to insist they pretend they do.

Chapter 13

THE CALCULUS OF
COMPASSION

I looked through the orange booklet with bolded letters on the cover SENIOR SERVICE PROJECT, and I placed my finger on the site I really wanted. There was an after-school program that didn't require us to report until 2 P.M. I fantasized about sleeping in and video game final levels where big bosses that yelled and shook the screen would finally see defeat. I'm talking to you, Donkey Kong!

As our twelfth grade Calculus teacher sat on her stool, she said, "You know, the Regis High School Senior Service Project is one of the most important things we offer. I know, you think serving others for a month will be a nice break from school, and it certainly will be. However, what you don't realize is that you can find your purpose if you let it. Take this one seriously, boys," Miss Koster said. If she spoke, I listened. She changed my path as a student and insisted I eat lunch with her every day until my grade in Geometry went from a D to an A.

Yup! She was not the teacher anyone could escape when it came to expectations.

My grades went from a 2.3 to a 3.8 in one semester, and my parents freaked out. My mother thought I was being kicked out of school when the dean's letter arrived in the mail, so finding out I was on the Dean's List was proof that it only takes one adult to change the life of a child. So, when Miss Koster expressed her opinion, I listened with a different ear.

As the bell rang, I tried to run out of there with the quarters in my hand ready to use the payphone so I could be the first to get my name on the list.

"Brian! Can you stay for a bit? I'll write you a note so you can be late to class," Miss Koster called out just before I could make my escape.

I quickly made my way to her desk and I tried to balance my expression with "How can I help, favorite teacher of all time?" and "I've got to pee really bad!".

She asked, "Do you need the restroom first?" Just like that, my harried expression failed. I knew this was a long chat. She looked at the chair I'd sat in more times than I could count. I knew there was no universe where I could run across the school, make a call, and then race back within any amount of time that would not create suspicion, and Miss Koster always knew when the truth left the room. She could sense it.

"Nope. I'm good. So, what's going on, Miss Koster? Was I talking too much during class? I didn't throw the spitball, but I'm not sure who did – Jerry did it. Okay, Mikey was also involved. But I didn't really get too involved. Well, I threw it back to Mikey after he hit my desk. It's really unsanitary, and it's not my fault. You see, …"

Miss Koster smiled and leaned back in her chair while she ran her tongue over the large upper front teeth that always had some green vegetable lodged in the largest buck teeth I had ever seen. She finally broke the silence of this inquisition by saying, "Oh Dear Lord! Well, that was a lot. I actually asked you to stay because I have a placement, I want you to consider. I think you'd be perfect."

I stumbled over my words, and I finally replied, "Well, I've got a placement picked out. It's the after-school program in Denver Public Schools near Five Points. It seems like a perfect fit for me."

She folded her arms across her chest, and she said, "Really? What called you about their program? I can't wait to hear."

"Well, I really liked the…. kids being… well, you know? The kids being in the after-school part seemed pretty amazing, and the after-school part was something that has great things for kids."

Miss Koster then realized she had me. It was her damn eyes and those scary as hell buckteeth smiling as the bits of salad that clung to the cliffs of her overbite finally succumbed to the force of her purpose. She finally said, "I can tell you've really thought this one through. I heard "kids" and then I think you said "kids" a few more times, which is great. The placement I want you to consider is The Children's Hospital of Denver. You're the perfect person for that assignment, and Sheila Dunn, their volunteer director, is so excited to meet you this Friday at 3:30 P.M. You won't let me down, will you?"

I replied, "No, Miss Koster. I will be there, but I really think the afterschool…"

Miss Koster wrote out a pass that looked like Sanskrit and stood up to let me know our little chat was finished. "Thank you, Brian. I'm so grateful you're willing to serve wherever you are most needed. That is the point of the project, and I am so grateful that you have embraced the spirit of this rite of passage."

I could only say the obligatory, "Thank you, Miss Koster," as I fled from the all-knowing eyes.

"Oh! By the way, spit wads are the reason you'll be in detention this afternoon. I'm just grateful you came clean. I'm shocked I didn't even notice. Mikey and Jerry will be joining you. It is in Mike Dougherty's office today. I believe it's "Clean Off Gum Underneath the Desk" day."

With that, I met with the volunteer director at Children's Hospital in Denver, and she started our supposed interview with, "Well, Miss Koster and myself are good friends, and she is so excited about you doing your senior project with us. Do you have any questions for me?" I left her office with my interview shirt Miss Koster insisted I use when I got to school on Friday. She was that teacher that didn't let you fail. I've come to realize this is how gay teachers love gay students. Words are never spoken, but her love for me never made sense. She insisted a different destiny meet my feet than the one my fear pretending to be laziness chose.

"Brian, can you take the book cart today? You're ready to be with the kids," Sheila said.

It had been three days, and she had observed us interacting with the kids in the daycare where the healthy siblings would be left when the parents were there to visit the kids. I had the kids make blanket forts and we played a lily pad game with carpet squares where I was the lava monster. We had so much fun, and I assumed we would be there the entire time. There were three others from my school, but I was the first to be sent into the hospital. It was one of my first times in life where I recognized I had a gift to offer.

I took the book cart everywhere. Sheila would give me a list of floors with kids' names and told me to check-in with the nursing station first. From there, I was starting a three-week adventure that would change the course of my life. I worked with Thomas, an eight-year-old boy with osteo sarcoma cancer who left the hospital after two weeks; I had never felt a joy like that in my life. My buddy Nicholas was a two-year old kiddo with significant physical challenges that kept him tied to the hospital his entire life. He lived in the ICU and I always wanted to rescue him whenever the nurse came like clockwork after his lunch to take his blood to ensure his organs were working.

Harrison, a twelve-year old with burns over more than 60 percent of his body, was in a private room and there was a metallic tub in the adjacent room where he was scrubbed daily with sponges that looked like steel wool. They called it "debriding", and his screams haunted me when he begged me to stay with him during his treatment. I wasn't allowed to be in the room, but I sat in the chair by the door and used my voice to reassure him.

In our weekly meeting on Friday, Sheila asked me in front of the other three students a question I have spent my life trying to answer.

"Brian, can you explain to the other students why it is you are comfortable going into any child's room? Nothing seems to make you uncomfortable."

I replied, "I don't know. It's not that hard. I'm just reading books."

Being sensitive and loving these beautiful children didn't look cool, so I did what I could to take the focus off of me and grew as quiet and disinterested as possible. I knew what Sheila said was true, but I didn't know why. The world often told me my sensitivity was a burden and if I'm honest, the journey of an empath is an exhausting one for the people who love us at times.

My sensitivity was often focused on how the world had failed me and how alone I felt which made me, at times, very self-centered and enamored with my own pain. This experience was demonstrating to me how that natural sensitivity could help me to witness those around me and be present to their suffering. By placing that sensitivity on others, I could be responsive to the child in front of me and know the role they needed me to play. Responding to whatever awaited me in those rooms felt natural.

That was until I met Violet.

The nurse at the Oncology station saw me approach, and she said, "Brian, Sheila needs you to give her a call. You can use this line."

I grabbed the phone, and Sheila said, "I need you to go the third floor and go to the nurse's station and ask to relate to Violet. Violet can't get comfortable today, and all they need you to do is hold her. She's only 8 months old, but she has dwarfism. She is the smallest child I have ever seen. Don't let all of the tubes and cords scare you. The lead nurse is expecting you."

I grabbed the book cart, and Sheila called out, "You won't need that, Brian. You will just be holding her."

As I got to the third floor, the lead nurse Miss Carver walked me into Violet's room, and said, "I'll be back to get you set-up soon. Make sure you use the restroom, because we typically sit with her for at least an hour. Her mom will be coming up after work from Colorado Springs. She can only be with her for a couple hours a day, so we need to fill in for her mom. Touch is so important with developing babies."

As I got closer to the crib, I looked inside, and I saw the most beautiful baby I had ever seen. However, she was clearly in pain. Her entire body was clenched, and her fists were tightly wound. You could see in her eyes that she was desperate and reaching out with all her strength.

However, not a sound escaped her agony.

Miss Carver said, "Brian, do you see how her trachea fills with steam? When you are sitting with her, I need you to use this blue bulb syringe to extract the sputum and fluid that collects. Her lungs are not fully developed, so she keeps getting these severe respiratory infections. The yellow bag is some very powerful antibiotics, and we're hoping this one wipes it out."

As she left, I stood over Violet, and I had never seen so many wires, clear tape on her hands, a yellow trap over her trachea filling with steam every time she clenched her fists, and machines beeping on all corners of her crib. I placed my hand on her chest, and I watched as her face immediately softened. I stared at her, and her eyes met mine. Everything in me reached to her, but I froze. I was so awkward in certain ways, and I imagined all the ways I would fail the most fragile creature I had ever met. I started feeling dizzy and seeing stars just as Miss Carver entered.

Miss Carver said, "Brian, you need to sit down. You're white as a sheet."

I quickly searched my database for the easiest lie to cover this moment when the freeze visited. It had happened in the past, and I became better at recovering to avoid the questions people ask when they know an emotional reaction is the cause of the breakdown.

I said, "I'm so sorry. I'm very hypoglycemic, and I didn't have time to eat breakfast. I'd better get someone else to take my place."

Miss Carver brought me some apple juice and I walked to the elevators. I didn't want to leave Violet, but I didn't trust myself. I had met the door where my courage and conviction failed me. I was so embarrassed that I let the team believe I was coming down with something, and my mother collected me as she had done so many times in my early schooling years to rescue me from moments when anxiety gripped my purpose.

Monday morning of the following week came, having spent the entire weekend being haunted by Violet's face. I imagined holding the blue bulbous syringe in my left hand as I anchored her with my right hand. It became clear walking in her room and trusting the unknown was my next step.

I came in twenty minutes early, and asked Sheila, "Can I plan to be with Violet today?"

Sheila said, "I was going to have Jeremy work with her today. Did you eat breakfast today?"

I replied, "Yes. I am in great shape."

Sheila said, "Miss Carver was hoping you'd give it another chance. Plan to be there at 10:30 A.M. I'll tell Miss Carver to expect you."

As I sat in the rocking chair in the corner, Miss Carver scooped up Violet in one hand and carried her over to me. I could once again see the anguish and restriction every muscle in her body demanded the world of voices and giants hear.

She placed her exactly how she needed to be, and Violet and I immediately locked eyes. Violet softened into my chest as Miss Carver reattached certain cords and reset certain machines that started beeping.

As Miss Carver left, Violet and I were linked in a way I had never experienced. If I smiled, she did too. I tickled her feet and she smiled with glee. The trach filled with steam as I placed my hand on her chest to anchor her. I then sang to her. It was a Mommas and Poppas song my mother played on the phonograph so many times I knew every word.

"Puff the Magic Dragon" was softly offered to her as she fell asleep in my arms. Miss Carver brought me apple juice every thirty minutes without fail, and I politely drank them down with the straw she gingerly placed in my mouth. My lie had consequences, but this moment made it all worth it. Violet and I became very close that day, and my mother was called to let her know I couldn't leave until Violet's mother arrived.

Chapter 14

BOOK CLUB FOR TWO

As I stormed into the office lunchroom where I was working as a person serving families without housing in a public school district, I saw an office mate Sandy sitting there by herself reading a book.

I asked, casually, "So, what book are ya reading? Is it a romance or a mystery?"

"It's about the Holocaust," Sandy replied, hoping I would know to leave her alone on her break.

She clearly doesn't know me, so I sat down across from her.

"What inspired you to read about the Holocaust?," I asked her.

Sandy removed her eyes from her book for the first time, recognizing her subtle communication to ignore her would be ignored completely by me.

"Well, I'm Jewish. These books are strangely powerful for me, and they inspire me. Also, my husband's side of his family lost so many during the Holocaust that I have felt drawn lately to reading as many books as I can find on the topic."

Sandy, at the time, was the budget technician capable of managing millions of dollars on her multiple spreadsheets, but she preferred her silence over humans a lot of the time. She took her work so seriously, so my enthusiastic rabid Carebear can be off-putting for most introverts, even though they soon realize I'm just pretending to be an extrovert.

Her grey hair with intense waves, even though it is short, draw your eyes to her. Even through her black plastic framed glasses, I saw a new version of Sandy. I saw some of the kindest eyes I had ever seen staring back at me.

It all started with her simple but powerful, "Yes. I'd be happy to have you join me." Her affirmation felt tremulous and protective. I knew it was a YES I would need to earn, and I could feel the vulnerable waters we were both choosing to travel as the world around us disappeared.

The Book Club for Two began that day. As we read a few books, we started to both protect the boundaries of our world, letting the world around us know we were not currently looking for other members and likely never would be.

Our first book was the famous Elie Wiesel's "Night" and one of his other less well-known works. We also read the courageous journey of Kitty Hart and I will never forget the moment when Kitty was breathing through the holes of the floor in a railcar as the allies were ascending. The Nazis sought to murder as many Jews as possible when they knew the war was all but lost. Kitty lost so much but she found a way to accept the air available through the holes of the floor until the allies opened the doors to her freedom. We read "The Zookeeper's Wife" about a zoo in Warsaw, Poland that became a hiding place for Jewish families. We also read of French families being forced together in a large domed outdoor park to then be sent off to the concentration camps.

For me, it was reading the book "The Men with the Pink Triangle" that shocked me even further. The cruelty and venomous hatred of men like me revealed stories less well-known and in no way less disturbing than the others we had read.

When we discussed this book, I will never forget Sandy with tears filling her eyes, saying, "How did our world ever allow such cruelty to be visited upon any person? This is your history, Brian. Now, maybe, we have discovered the reason you and I have gone on this journey together."

We wept with these narrators and silently agreed to carry their stories on our hearts and minds for the rest of our days as a small way of honoring what is possible when we allow ourselves to see one another as anything other than mirrors of the other.

I was forced to reckon with my memories of antisemitic words I had used against a Jewish student attending our Catholic elementary school. How did I know those words would hurt him the most? Where did I even learn to hate in such a particular way as a young person?

When I shared this memory, Sandy said, "Brian, you were a child. You were taught that your religion and your culture was superior. It's important to remember our country is still learning this lesson. Any calendar will tell you just much Christian holidays are taken on as national holidays. Any school calendar will prove this. You were a white Catholic young man with blonde hair and blue eyes, and now, you are learning to see through many different eyes. Isn't that beautiful?"

I asked, "So, Sandy, is being Jewish a religion, a culture, or a race?"

She answered, "Yes!"

#

"Don't order the breadsticks. They are a cheesy mess. Just do the pizza here. It's Heaven," my Uncle John said. At the time, he had a body like Santa Claus with his deep-set eyes and black and silver hair. He had been a Republican House member in the state of Colorado and was an amazing entrepreneur.

We hadn't seen him and his wife for many years, because of conflicts he had with my mother. However, we had always gotten along. So, when he reached out, John and I set a time to meet for a meal at one of his favorite Italian places. After all, my Uncle John and his wife were some of the only relatives that attended our gay wedding over twenty years ago. I would never forget this kindness.

"Uncle John, you'd mentioned you had something you wanted to share with me. What's up?," I asked.

His wife Carol then took a spiral-bound booklet from inside a manila envelope and handed it to me. Carol then said, "Well, there's no quick way to explain all of this. I've recently gotten into genealogy…"

My uncle interrupted her, saying, "She's become obsessed with all things ancestors. It's become quite a hobby."

Carol laughed a bit, and then continued, saying, "Well, we discovered your family is Jewish. Your mother's dad was one hundred percent Jewish, and we even found gravestones located in Saint Louis, Missouri where your mother grew up in the heart of the Jewish cemetery."

I looked through the picture booklet of images of the SINGER name and saw headstones and old black and white pictures that tried to fill in the holes of a big part of our family story. I'd only ever known the Catholic rituals of faith and I attended Catholic schools all the way through my master's degree.

My uncle's voice broke me out of my inner world, asking, "So, how's your mom doing these days?"

"Uncle John, she's not well. She's in the nursing home, and she's frankly getting worse every day."

Explaining my mother's journey into the nursing home felt like a betrayal of my family secrets, so I repeated the story of my mother likely having Alzheimer's, but the truth was a much harder tale to honor. Her addiction to benzos and an anxiety disorder that often left her trapped in the confines of her bedroom became the altar by which a gay son approaches his mother. As she smoked her Marlboro Reds, the rings of smoke and conversations we had always amazed me.

However, to find her, you needed to cross over the rivers of depression and ancient anxieties to find her territory. Over time, her body matched the weight of her insides, and she started to have these scary episodes when she would overdose on her medications.

After repeated episodes, she would no longer be aware of time and space. She would sometimes not recognize me in these haunted forests and my eyes could not find her. She was lost in an abyss of memories, and her brain was trying to weave back together enough neurons to reclaim consciousness. After these episodes, she would return for a while and then she would be once again claimed into the underworld of her traumas.

Over my lifetime, my mother would always talk about the day her father died when she was only seventeen years old.

One day, when I went to see her, she said, "Do you know if my daddy will find me? I am so scared he is lost."

In this moment, at a local Italian restaurant with red and white checkered placemats and more sauce than pizza, I was finally hearing the world of my mother's father. It almost felt as if I had found him finally, and I could begin to bring her the pieces of him so she could once again be whole.

"Thank you, Uncle John! Weirdly, this kinda makes sense. Did you know when you were a child? Do you remember anything?"

He replied, "Yes. It was a part of us we never shared. It was a private part that faded over time."

#

Unfortunately, my fantastical idea betrayed the arc of her story. She would die soon after that conversation. I believe it was roughly three months.

Sometimes, stories in life don't end the way we plan. I'd always, on some level, hoped I would be the person to rescue my mother from the darkness of her past. I began to understand that her story is a powerful one, even if the ending isn't the stuff of fairytales. Her ending is true and she is a teacher to any willing to see the courage and tenacity her life asked of her.

After my mom died, I was given a great opportunity to facilitate a grief group for other LGBTers at the local community center. We all became very close, and the process of allowing grief to speak back to us became a powerful bonding experience.

One day, one of the members who was becoming a friend, Eddie, called me and said, "You Know, Brian. I'm a Jew. I need your help here. I can't find any rabbi willing to come to my place for my husband's memorial service to read the Kaddish. That's the prayer we say, as Jews, when a loved one has died. I don't know what to do."

His pain and anguish filled the phone as the waves of sobs broke free. This pain of grief for his husband against the backdrop of knowing his religion of childhood and cultural identity was not willing to join him in his river of sorrow.

I kept picturing him standing alone in this river and the rabbis refusing to reach for him.

That's when I called Sandy.

"I would be honored to come and read the Kaddish Prayer at the ceremony. Nothing would make me happier. At some point, I chose to honor the over six million empty chairs over the voice of authority. Love needs to win at some point, don't you think?" I then remembered the black and white photo of her husband, Howard's ancestors. This black and white photo of many family members taken in the forties reflected over half the faces dying in the Holocaust.

Sandy showed up and read the words in Hebrew as Eddie wept into the ethers, hoping his beloved would hear the words.

As with all religious prayers, there are alternate interpretations. For me, I believe this is a prayer for the person in mourning and reaching out to God directly to ask that the world be as holy as we imagine God to be. More importantly, the mourner is asking that the brokenness of the world and our failure to love one another as God does be healed. It is a prayer that asks God to honor the suffering of life and to pray that the world reflect the greatness and magnificence of God's love, honoring that our world is not there yet.

There will be many that will disagree with my interpretation, and I am no biblical scholar. However, I'm kinda thinking ancient script can be offered new eyes and awareness.

I only know that Sandy became an ambassador of the love that we are promised exists in the eyes of God for all her children. She chose to recite a prayer for a person in mourning and, in doing, she brought the Jewish culture that Eddie knew and loved into the center of his grief.

Her very presence extended to him in the rapids of his sorrow and showed me the very possibility of a loving God the Kaddish Prayer invokes.

I also know that the coincidences of a chance encounter in a lunchroom allowed that moment to prevail, and I will never be able to honor the power of this moment properly.

I can only say that I have come to see the hand of God in the hands of so many people that reach to me in my sorrows or confusion or fear.

I may never be Jewish in the real sense, and I know I am twenty-five percent Ashkenazi Jew, according to 23 and Me. That somehow helps me to know that twenty-five percent of me belongs to the same world that created a soul such as Sandy. That means the fifty-percent of my mother that saw her ancestry in the eyes of her loving father has returned to her in her death. However, with these identities, how is one to find wholeness?

The identities somehow become irrelevant, because I saw what happened when someone abandoned the rules of their culture to reach into the waters of a person in grief and offer a loving witness. Sandy saw only a person in need and the eyes of the rabbis that rejected this offer could only see the identities that separate us.

Grief doesn't care about your beliefs. If you're breathing, you are companioning with grief every day. Sandy showed me what can occur when we are reaching to something greater in the moments that really matter.

Grief is the universal river and I'm over some pretending they are never wet. When you've known the pain and sorrow of grief that exists in lamentations and elegies in every language, we come to find the single language and common ground we discover in veterinarian's offices or airport arrival areas.

I want to be the person reaching into the river with both of my hands and seeing a person suffering as my sister or my brother.

I want to be more like you, Sandy.

I want to hold tightly to the parts of me the world judges to stand for others who feel alone in the desert seeking belonging and abandon any identity that separates me from the needs and pain of others.

Isn't this the greatest lesson of honoring the empty chairs? We recognize we cannot change the ending, but can we at least honor the weight of the sacrifice their life extends to every soul?

Chapter 15

THE JOURNEY OF A YES

I remember when I met Nash. He was a thin toy poodle who looked like a used puppet, all of six pounds, shivering in a metal cage and refusing to touch an overflowing bowl of food. He smelled like shit and fresh urine. He was frozen.

A dog person knows. We have some strange genetic fate that brings a creature like this onto our path. Cat people understand this propensity too. You're just standing there in a Pet Smart getting food for your other furry companions when a moment like this occurs. Or, you're simply minding your own business when suddenly, a thought occurs that you should head on over to the local animal shelter (after perusing their website for days) and select a new friend. All animal lovers know we are the powerless in this exchange. The animal chooses us, and we only need to say "Yes."

A wizened older dog person knows the power of that moment. As I was minding my own business in the line at Pet Smart, purchasing a new dog bed for Miss Lily, a husky woman with a name tag that said

MANAGER approached me. I thought to myself that either her parents had high expectations, or they'd never heard of a baby name book.

Then, she said, "I'm Carla, the manager. I have a dog I need you to meet. He is perfect for you. Trust me."

I can't say No to a person with the word MANAGER on her name tag. I am a good Catholic boy after all.

"Look at him. Isn't he so cute?" she said. Before looking in his cage, I was already doing the inner eyeroll that I did with the nuns behind their back. Then, I looked in the cage, and the "Yes" was there immediately. It was like the moment in West Side Story when Tony sees Maria from across a crowded dance hall, and the love is instantaneous. The dog belonged to me, and I belonged to him. Just like that. Our souls were waiting for the other.

Carla the Manager: Would you like to hold him?

Me: Uh, I better not. My husband has asked that we not get another dog, and we really...

Carla the Manager: Are you sure? He's really sweet.

Me: Well, okay.

Carla the Manager: Let's have you go into this little area over here, and we'll bring him to you.

Brian (thinking): Oh crap! What was I going to do? If he came to meet me, the love would be impossible to deny. I was already choosing customized dog beds and fancy dog biscuit flavors to share. John is going to kill me! There's no way.

Carla the Manager: Sit here and look sideways as I place him in your lap. He's scared, as you can tell.

Brian: What's his story?

Carla the Manager: His name is Wyatt. He was the stud in an illegal puppy mill in Fort Lupton, and he lived in a cage outside at a ranch until they decided to get rid of them. They've worked out a partnership with this non-profit, and the agency collects the dogs when they are no longer useful. He's a purebred chocolate toy poodle. Do you know how expensive they are to buy? He's like a designer dog.

That's always been my secret goal—to carry a little toy dog that matches my pink hair. Not!

She placed him in my lap as I sat cross-legged on the floor. Wyatt looked at me and shook like a leaf. I've never seen an animal shake that way. I was speechless. I used my hand to pull him gently close to my stomach. I used my other hand to make little circles behind his ears and neck.

He wouldn't look at me. His eyes remained frozen as his nervous system created waves of anxiety through every nerve ending.

I was blown away. My undeniable connection with Wyatt formed words that made it to the tip of my tongue. Wyatt and I both heard my first words to him as I said the most powerful thing a person says in a moment like this: "Yes."

It was never a choice. The soul speaks louder than the human mind (which exists in a universe of lack and worry).

In that moment, Wyatt peed. He didn't move as the puddle spread to the pads of his back feet.

Carla stepped in and scooped him up in her arms. "He's clearly not house broken."

We both knew that wasn't the real issue. No, he's just broken, because no one has offered him a home.

I've learned a powerful truth about my husband, John. If he knows something is really, really important, he never stands in my way. After tears started flowing, his "Yes" joined mine. We were now both committed to adopting a seven-pound toy poodle. After having us fill out paperwork and agreeing to a house visit to ensure we weren't serial killers and our fence height was higher than 12 inches (roughly Wyatt's height), we were told we could collect him at that same Pet Smart that Saturday, fully neutered and vaccinated. It would be seven days apart from him, and I missed him already. I even called on that Wednesday to see how he was doing.

We arrived right when they opened, and the adoption counselor from Every Creature Counts sat down in an office with us. His name was Henry. He asked us, respectfully, to consider the weight of this decision.

As was clearly obvious, he said, "Wyatt is a special-needs kind of dog. I need to know you mean "Yes". Many think they can take home a dog like this, and all will be well. That is not the case here. He's been in our care for almost three months, and we've never found a good placement. Are you sure?"

I felt as if he was describing me. I was the fag walking the streets of Washington DC hoping for a friendly couch with no other agendas and I could see the pain of not being claimed in his eyes. The "Yes" people offered in my life felt like the same weight and I could recall so many memories of how I had failed that love people offered. I looked across the table to Henry, and I looked him in the eyes. I insisted he feel the "Yes" this occasion offered. I was never more certain of anything.

Henry said, "I'm not convinced Wyatt can recover. He's been through a lot and has never been handled. Are you sure you want to take this dog home?"

I looked at him and said, "Wyatt is not staying here, because he has a new life when he leaves this place. He will forever be Nash because his new life insists on a new name." My hubby came up with the name because Crosby, Stills, and Nash was on the radio when we decided to adopt Nash. It fit. It was a one syllable name with a soft -sh sound. Could we quiet the past just by using a softer name?

Henry quietly signed his name to the form, and the adoption was approved. It was that simple, but the complex journey Nash and I would take was just beginning.

#

Carla the Manager: (Greeting us as we exited) I'm so grateful you have a new friend in your life. You're so lucky to have him. He will change you. I just know it.

Me: Don't you mean he's lucky to have us? We're the ones that are rescuing him.

If you say so. I've always believed the right dog finds us when we need them most. I'm just grateful you said "Yes!"

When he peed in the bed and on the floor and on the couch multiple times while shaking, we both said "Yes."

When he bit us multiple times whenever we lifted him up after he tried to run away, we said "Yes."

When he pooped blood the first time he learned to walk on a leash, we said "Yes."

When he shivered all night in fear during a thunderstorm while camping at Ponderosa State Park in Idaho, I held him close to me, singing a lullaby I would sing many times (including the very day we had to say goodbye to him). I sang that "Yes."

It's the moment he first said Yes that everything changed.

He was placed in bed with us from the first night he arrived. Lily would climb under all of the covers and attach herself to me or to John's stomach and not move all night.

However, Nash found the farthest corner of the bed as far from us as possible that first night, and he panted. He panted and panted and panted. We'd awake in the morning with Nash resting his little head off the corner of the bed unable to find an escape from this prison of blankets. His eyes would be staring off as we started our morning ritual.

Over a couple of months, he stayed fixed in that corner. I covered him with a small grey and light blue flannel blanket and made gentle circles behind his ears every night. He remained fixed to that far corner of the bed looking confused and exhausted.

One evening, I woke to do my middle-of-the-night-business (including ravaging some form of sweet from the cupboard). As I returned to bed, Nash was standing at my pillow waiting for me. I sat on the side of the bed and pulled him close to me and rubbed him behind his ears. I crawled back into bed, and he rested against my legs. He used my legs as a backboard to relax more than he ever had, releasing a long breath. He traveled from my legs to my stomach and then eventually to the spot he claimed for six years at my neck and chest. He always had to be on the outside of the bed and that never changed.

Nash said Yes.

He never bit us again, but the shivering and the eyes of fear still gripped him at times. Sudden movements or loud noises still made him shake and shiver. He sought me out in those moments. He would wake me in the night to get on my side, and I'd pull him close as he stared off, waiting for his frenzied thoughts to calm.

Some fear never quiets. It existed in a hidden place within him that no amount of love or touch or patience or compassion could vanquish.

Maybe, that's true for all of us. That panic, that freeze, that grip still visits me. I can't always see the fingerprint of the memories visiting from the past, but the terror is real, knowing no time or place.

Nash reflected me, and I reflected him. Who was the healer, and who was the broken one? Who was the leader, and who was the follower?

After more than seven years of Nash being in my life, I had gone from working full-time to being on disability for a brain issue that causes unrelenting headaches and keeps me from being able to operate a vehicle from time to time. The serious part of that journey and two surgeries all launched within six weeks of Nash becoming our companion.

He was the sentry on the corner of the couch, standing guard as Lily and I cuddled, and I moved in and out of consciousness, slowly emerging from the procedure or another headache. Nash protected me, took naps with me, licked me on my neck for hours upon hours when I was unable to get out of bed, and even cried with me in the wee hours when sleep wasn't possible. Lily and Nash, in my new world of isolation, had become the comfort and connection that kept me hopeful and reminded me of my purpose.

When I picked up my phone to do a reading, Nash and Lily took their positions as the work began. They held the container as mothers and sons and daughters and fathers, and friends used the energy of our love to share a message and light a lantern of hope for their remaining loved one. Our love became the sanctuary for Spirit—and all of us were the mediums.

#

"It's the fair thing to do. It really is. He's suffering." Her veterinarian training on offering words of guidance to people in this moment felt rehearsed and forced, but I knew it was time. I knew before those words escaped her lips. She needed to let me know she understood, and she was also agreeing to share the burden of this moment.

This is that time when my Yes had to be tested. Was Nash's quality of life and suffering going to win over my desire to hold him here and to ask him to participate in my complete and utter denial of how bad things had gotten?

This is another lesson of the Yes. I hate this lesson. Can I love someone until it hurts like hell and be the gentle hand and pay the ferryman for his journey across that wide river to the other side? Can I love him enough to stand on the side of that shore and wish him well on his next journey?

He never belonged to me anyhow. He was never mine.

As he lay there with his head raised, I looked at him, and his eyes said Yes.

Those deep pools in his brown eyes were covered in a cataract gauze that looked like moons from another world. I stared into those eyes, eyes that could barely see the world he inhabited. It was clear. His eyes said Yes.

So, I simply joined his Yes.

After she injected the anti-anxiety shot, Nash made a pained whimper.

He slowly became heavier and heavier, and then, after a minute, he started to weave side to side. Before he collapsed, He lunged for my arm and rested his head on my arm.

He let go with a long sigh. I was not expecting it. His eyes were open, his tongue was hanging out of his mouth. I gently made circles in the fur behind his ears.

I said "I love you," over and over again. Nash was gone.

A few minutes passed, and the veterinarian returned. She injected a pink solution into Nash's back leg. I knew that pink color. You never imagine death traveling on the waves of a pink liquid, but in a vet's office that color always tells the tale.

I wept into Nash's ear and continued making circles in his fur even after I knew he was gone.

Then, a hovering softness like warm water poured through me. I have come to know this sensation well...Nash's soul travelled through the center of my heart.

He was on to his way to a new adventure, leaving smoke signals in an unseen sky.

#

I am staring at Nash's shell now. His life no longer has limits. His light permeates well beyond the walls of this sterile office with its humming fluorescents. I see a white coat. The body in it leads me into the reception area. I'm walking in a kind of mist. I smell rubbing alcohol. I hear condolences from strangers. A clerk takes my credit card, shakes my hand, and ushers me out the door.

I turn around one last time. I can see into the office where Nash's body rests. The grey and blue plaid flannel throw is covering him.

Is that really Nash? Is it really done?

Was Nash's final gasp one of release, or one of terror?

If I'm honest, I believe fear led the way, but I know peace won.

In the journey of death, peace always wins.

#

What does the journey of a Yes teach us then?

Why do we say Yes?

My friend Art's lungs filled with fluid as his pneumonia slowly kept the oxygen from reaching the air sacs in his lungs. Hemoglobin was trying to reach the molecules of oxygen, but the fluid of his ravenous disease was winning. Scott O died in his sleep, likely from a heart attack. My dear Angel was found on the floor after a severe seizure. And my mother, ravaged with a long partnership with pain and anxiety and a milky spine from osteoporosis officially died. Her diminished reality and her dementia took her from me long before death ever did.

This is where Yes changes.

Am I willing to live in a world without these souls and smiles and hearts and friends?

When they passed, the lessons each of them held (lessons that had always pointed in the direction of love) also died. The human words dripped and floated away before landing on earth as final goodbyes and sweet memories.

Am I willing to live in this world?

This Yes is different because the answer is not as clear as I might wish. It is a chance once again to accept that healing mostly requires time. In our world of technology and fast-paced solutions, grief cannot be pushed ahead of its timeline. The clock of grief keeps time with a different rhythm and an altogether impossible calendar.

#

During my first reading after Nash's death, a lovely grandfather came to me and showed me his wonderful life on a farm. He cared for his milk cows, his crops, and his companion dog. He showed me special moments in the life of his granddaughter and how much his wife had meant to him.

At the end of the reading, Nash was in the arms of this grandfather, and he said, "You've got a great dog here, Brian. Don't worry. Angel is taking care of him. There is nothing to fear."

Angel was the very friend I had asked to greet Nash. My friend Angel was that strange person who barely belongs to the human experience, because her feet were rooted in a different earth and her soul was from a different time.

The memory of Nash's death haunted me. After a week of being awakened by a dream of Nash falling onto my arm and me not being able to revive him, the nightmare quieted. As I crawled into the bed with the soothing lullaby of the white noise machine filling the space, I felt Nash comforting me. He cuddled in the arc of my neck and filled me with warmth. Nash's presence turned the fears of the night into a lullaby. The thunder of grief quieted, and I could sleep through the night once again.

After John collected our dear Nash's remains from the veterinarian clinic, he placed the blue box they gave him on a shelf in the garage. One night at midnight, after watching too much news and being distracted by the voices of impending doom and fear, I decided to open the blue box. Inside were two velvet blue bags, both tied with a velvet drawstring. One was clearly Nash's ashes; the bag weighed little more than a pound. The second bag, however, was a mystery. As I unwrapped it, a ceramic circle fell into my hands.

I knew...I turned it over, and there was Nash's paw print. I wept as I held it close to my heart.

His small paw print was now a fossil. Nash really had been here. He really had been my friend and companion. He was real.

Even time couldn't take that truth away.

The man I was before Nash would never be the same as this man. That "Yes" left me a different soul. The love we had exchanged had forever changed me. I was a new person, with new feet and new eyes. Nash had forever changed me. He showed me that love heals all wounds.

I will never fully understand why the "Yes" we offer in love is also tied inextricably to loss. It does make this moment matter more. The colors are sharper, and the people I love will not be here forever. I also won't be.

Maybe this time, my Yes will mean even more than I could have ever imagined, because my Yes is wiser and softer and more hopeful than ever.

Yes. This three-letter word has changed my life more times than I care to mention.

But, in the words of My Wise Lesbian Yoda-Like Sister, 'I'm just grateful you said 'Yes!'

I am too, dear one.

Chapter 16

THE FAITHFUL FOREST

"Your kidneys are starting to improve, but we will be having our neurologist on staff come by later to discuss the findings on your MRI. We can see clearly why you've been having headaches," the doctor in her white lab coat said as she grabbed my hand. Rosanna was written in capital letters and many letters followed. Since I had entered the emergency room at Lutheran Hospital with double vision and imbalance five days prior, she had been the constant in the journey since being admitted.

"Well, that seems like good news. It sounds like they found the reason why you've been struggling the past four years," John said from the bright green velour chair that looked like a torture device. Wooden arms and faux leather that screeched with any movement announced his words as he leaned forward. John continued, saying, "Is that right, Doctor?"

Doctor Rosanne replied, "It's neither good nor bad. It's not cancer, but it is a real issue that will require attention throughout his life. It is a rare brain malformation, but it isn't a death sentence in any way. Doctor Reynolds will be by this afternoon to break it down for you," she said. I find being discussed as if I'm not in the room to be the most uncomfortable feeling in life. All I could hear was not a death sentence. My lower lungs filled with new oxygen as I took a deep breath, realizing Death had left the waiting room.

I replied, "Thanks Doc! Weirdly, it helps to know I'm not crazy."

She replied with her wry smile, "I didn't say you weren't crazy, but we just might have an explanation."

We laughed and I was grateful I'd found a doctor who knew how to work with me. She continued, saying as she looked right into my eyes, "New information can be scary, but I have come to trust that whatever health issue we manage in this life, it serves us. You get to feel sorry for yourself for a little while, but you are going to walk out of here with your whole life staring at you. You're twenty-nine years old, and you have many decades of life ahead of you. As you learn more about this condition and the challenges it may offer you, please don't lose sight of what this can teach you. In many ways, my life began after I was diagnosed with breast cancer. I've never been happier than I am now. Can you trust me on this one?"

I nodded in approval, but it irritated me that she went all 'self-help book' on me when I didn't even know what the diagnosis was. I was in 'whiny-butt mode', and I was not ready to be in 'enlightened spiritual master' mode, not just yet. Besides, it's a lot to ask a young gay man with his ass hanging out in a drab not even close to cerulean blue gown on to be insightful and thoughtful about a new diagnosis. I asked for extra tapioca pudding and whined to anyone in a uniform that was willing to listen.

I needed to at least attend my pity party first, and then I'd embrace my inner Gandhi and get on with it.

For four days, I was walking around in a gown with my bum hanging out and urinating in a large plastic bucket to look for protein in my urine. I was getting poked every twelve hours to check my creatinine to see if the kidneys were starting to improve, but my reason for going to the ER was due to having double vision on the highway with a searing headache that felt like a hand of nails gripping my neck and head. My high creatinine numbers caused them to focus on the kidneys, but they finally did a contrast dye MRI on the third afternoon to assess the original issue.

As the neurologist Doctor Reynolds explained the condition, they then suggested I be transferred immediately for brain surgery at a local hospital. John made a loud screeching sound in the green chair as he leaned forward, saying, "We're not rushing this. If he's not dying, can we just get him home after this kidney piece and then see the specialist?" I was so shocked to see my meek and low-key hubby react so intensely.

Doctor Reynolds looked at John and said, "If that's what you both think is best, we can ensure he sees the specialist soon after he is released from the hospital. This is a very serious issue however, so this is not something that can be tabled. Besides, we're starting to think Brian using Ibuprofen daily is the very reason his kidneys are failing. He cannot continue as he has for the last four years."

I replied, "You do realize I mentioned this headache issue to my doctor for over four years, and she kept telling me I was stressed."

Doctor Reynolds replied, "Well, it's time to get a new doctor, because this is not caused by stress. This is likely a genetic issue, but we just don't know. It is a rare abnormality, so we can't address the many questions I'm sure you have."

John said, "That's our first step. He's never going to be seen by her again. We'd appreciate any suggestions."

Doctor Reynolds replied, "Absolutely. I hear all the time from patients how they have felt embarrassed or ashamed to keep telling their doctor that the issue they are dealing with has not resolved or been clarified in any way. You deserved better."

I replied, "We all do. Every one of us deserves better. If you don't care about someone's pain, you shouldn't be allowed to wear that coat."

The triple-board certified neurologist accepted these words with a gentle smile, seeming to understand both the fear and grief that inspired it. Dr. Reynolds then said, "I'm sorry, but you won't be going home today. We need to keep you one more day to complete a kidney biopsy so we ensure we have done everything we can to ensure this issue was truly caused by Ibuprofen use."

I looked at John in his screeching chair and cried. He joined me. We knew that this magical mystery tour of life was not permanent. We also knew that we would need to be more to one another and grow our love to prepare for the roads that lie ahead for both of us. We both knew we were human and messy and imperfect. The myth had to die, so a new way of choosing love and one another could replace the fantasy.

The answers I had sought for over four years had finally arrived. I recognize how many other friends in my life who had been experiencing their own challenging health issues had not found the respect or compassion they deserved from the medical system and frankly, if I'm honest, from me. I often minimized people's pain and imagined I would have known exactly what to do if I had their situation.

As I laid in that bed for those seven nights, I was forced to acknowledge my own arrogance. I often imagined the circumstances of another person's journey had simple solutions that appeared obvious. Watching those replays in my mind that week in the quiet hum of machines and unbreakable routines with blood draws, morning tests, and lonely as hell nights showed me how my certainty in the face of another's complexity likely caused a lot of harm along the way. The lesson of this curriculum was already forcing different eyes to see the version of me the world knew versus the version of me I was hoping to become. That chasm in that moment felt impossible to bridge, but the challenge to be more decent towards others in pain and exercise my muscle of compassion felt like the real work I had managed to avoid all these years.

This was the week when I recognized my health would change everything about my life plan.

This was the week when my purpose began to matter more than your approval.

This was the week when I chose myself over my reputation.

This was the week when the seeds of mediumship could germinate into a purpose beyond anything my mind could have imagined at the time. I thought I was losing my identity, but, instead, I was shedding the lies and fears that felt like purpose.

This was the week when I ate more tapioca pudding than any other human being on the planet. I should have petitioned the Guinness Book of World Records because it is still one of my greatest accomplishments.

More than everything, I had finally become willing to become the person I told the world I was. I didn't say 'able'. I only said 'willing.' It's a journey, Y'all!

As I rested in that hospital bed for that week's stay, I was forced to look at who I was. I was in the middle of a doctoral program in Educational Leadership (YAWN!!!!), which I could not care less about. I knew that program no longer made any sense. My immortality died, and it was replaced with a purpose that had always been there, waiting for my urgency and ambition to quiet long enough to be acknowledged. In the quiet, once again, the grace that had saved me so many times embraced me.

I would need to choose between my victim and my purpose, because both don't fit in the backpack of life. There's only room for one.

I have chosen both at different times, and it has illuminated a profound lesson:

My victim always proves my drama, and the pity the world offers can still feel like love, but it will never be mistaken for grace.

However, my purpose always proves that I am a part of all living things, no better and no worse. I am in harmony with all living things, great and small. I belong to the river of life, and I am never alone in those rapids. I remember to love and offer the solace my soul needs, and somehow, I find the shore once again. The lessons learned in the dark become universal and teach me how to see and love every person that crosses my path. In other words, I'm on a journey to be the Care Bear I've always known I am but maybe a bit less rabid.

*

"Should we bring your walking stick?" John said, finally knowing the word "cane" was banished from his vocabulary. "Walking stick" made me feel like a wizened wizard ready to deny demons from the underworld passage into this world, even though the memory of my first dramatic fall occurred when walking our dogs. As I came back to consciousness, I will never forget the kind eyes of my ginger Viking with blue eyes asking if I was okay.

As we meandered through an Aspen grove covered in yellow robes with ornaments of burgundy occasionally, the eyes of aspens stare back at you through half-moons carved in black. I placed my demon destroyer stick on my outside arm to avoid upsetting our new rescue toy poodle - Nash, and the path winded through the freshly fallen leaves of autumn.

As the tree line ended, the craggy rock of Colorado tundra emerged. The afternoon wind had already picked up, but the intensity was turned up significantly as we stepped more and more into this zone of small bushes and larger rocks.

John grabbed my shoulders behind me and said, "Those are the trees we're here to see. They are called Methuselah Trees. They are the oldest type of tree in North America. They can live over five thousand years."

The tree looked like a miniature pine tree that God twisted twenty times, looking as if it was growing sideways. The small green needles reached to the Heavens as the tree branches looked like exhausted arms of an ancient boxer ready for one more round of winter.

I chose to stand with one tree and John joined me at my side. We both stood quietly and tried to imagine how this short tree with a wide trunk had survived the decades upon decades of seasons. I placed my hand on her trunk and felt the undulating waves that looked as if God herself reached down and twisted her in one direction. Her grey trunk twisted with the wind towards the distant blue sky well above timberline, where most trees disappear. These powerful sentinels of the forest gripped the ground with roots anchored to rocks and tundra. How they survived and lived for so many centuries is still, in many ways, a scientific mystery.

He continued, saying, "We also call it the Bristlecone Pine. Isn't it beautiful? If you look sideways, it gives you a sense of how much this tree has had to push against the intense non-stop winds of this ridge."

I asked, "Why does it grow in a twisted way? Does it help with it's roots in the hardened earth?"

He gripped my shoulders, saying, "Do you feel that?" As we stood there, the current of wind whistling across the edge of the mountain was constant and intense.

I replied, "Duh! It's freaking windy. The wind would come in multiple directions so that doesn't make sense." I traced my finger across her rivers of flow and tried to follow just one path from the top to the base. I couldn't. This tree has likely twisted in complete circles many times to withstand the forces of nature thrown her way. It was a wonder I likely would have missed all together if John had not included me in his world.

John said, "That's part of the mystery. I think it's cool that it chooses to twist in one direction, knowing, at times, it is with the wind and other times, pushing against it."

As I stood there with my cane, leaning on the trunk of my beloved, I couldn't determine if I was seeing her or if she was offering me a more compassionate way to see myself.

We were all connected in that moment, and the three of us stood in awe of the very gift of life itself. I knew the pathways of decades and the tribulations she experienced were present for all to see, and the only requirement was to notice.

I'm coming to realize that mediumship is the willingness to notice what is always there but often not seen. Mediumship requires only our presence, and the mysteries awaiting us as we trace the lines from the roots to the branches are endless. Some scars will be reflections of our own, and the chords of our very soul will know these stories as if they are our own, and other scars will offer a chance for the winds of another's journey to create footprints for future souls to follow. So, their stories can also be told through the resonance of our awareness.

I sometimes wonder if I would choose this life again, knowing that the pain and anguish of grief would be my greatest teacher. I had always been taught that my value was determined by my accomplishments in this human experiment, and, by that measure, I was never going to be enough. My ambitions and the chords of urgency played by fear could feel like my purpose. If only I could accomplish this or that or both this and that or this plus that and some more that and a lot more this, then I would truly know I mattered. I could know I was here, and I made my mark.

However, as I sat with this tree, her rivers of experience flowed and undulated over the valleys and mountains of history. I began to imagine the stories that every angle of her gentle but steadfast purpose would offer if her language could reach the syllables of mine.

My body was not failing me; It was teaching me.

It was reminding the ancient part of me that I am not my name, my accomplishments, my social capital, or my bank statements.

I am simply another leaf who forgot I am a part of every tree.

Chapter 17

MY DATE WITH DEATH

My watch flashed 1:59 P.M. as my phone vibrated with a calendar notification. I was right on time with a minute to spare. I walked into the fifties-themed diner named The Boardwalk well known for their gourmet meatloaf and Mac and Cheese that should be classified as a schedule 2 drug. Yes, it is that good. The signage made it clear this was a recreation of the perfect diner with walls covered in black and white checker patterns and neon lights highlighting their menu favorites.

"My name is Lorraine! Welcome to the Boardwalk Original Diner! Table for one?" Her smile was hidden, but there was no doubt she loved her job. Her curly red hair and bright red lipstick proved some styles never belong to a decade.

I replied, "Well, I'm meeting someone here. Her name is Izzie, and she's…"

Lorraine interrupted, "She's unforgettable. She is likely the nicest customer I've ever sat. I could tell her my life story, and weirdly, I think she'd actually give a shit."

Lorraine placed both of her hands on her mouth and stepped back, "I'm so sorry. I'm not normally such a potty mouth. I hope you will forgive me. This mask makes everything more awkward, ya know?"

I replied, "No worries. Don't you give it another thought. Has Izzie already arrived?"

Lorraine replied, as she departed with my menu above her head being carried as a flag in her right hand. "I'll take you to her now. She asked for a booth by the window, and she's already ordered a vanilla malt…"

I interrupted, saying, "Let me guess: Did she add some fries with a side of ranch?," I replied.

"Well, yes, she did. Your mother must be a lovely person."

I said, "Lorraine, she's not my mother. She's more of a mentor."

Lorraine replied, "Oh, I know. Aren't you lucky to get to be with Izzie?"

I replied, "I certainly am."

As I sat down across from Izzie, she reached for my hands and she held them in hers.

"You can take off your mask now," she said.

"Are you sure that's wise with you at the table?," I replied.

Izzie pursed her lips and rolled her eyes in a playful way as if she was offended by my inside joke, but then she looked at me. She looked at me in the eyes, and I recognized after only three meetings, we had become old friends. Maybe, we always had been.

She then sat back and the meeting had begun. Like that, it was down to business, almost professional in her focused shift.

Izzie said, "Hello, Dear One. Are we really just going to sit here or do you have a question you want me to answer?," she said as she continued to warm her hands and shift and shake trying to find the perfect middle of the cherry red booth that reflected the light with it's plastic sheen.

Thankfully, the song, "It's My Party, I Can Cry If I Want To" had finally ended. That genre of music makes me weirdly anxious, because you can never discern if the song is beginning or ending. How did anyone dance to that crap?

Her fee is a vanilla malt and French fries perfectly crisp with a side of ranch dressing for every meeting, and there are only a few restaurants that offer this heart-clogging combo. I don't know why I thought she would eat a salad. It kinda makes sense frankly.

Izzie continued, "Why are we meeting at 2 P.M. on November 21, 2020?"

I replied, "I have no idea. I just knew I needed to see you."

"Brian, you reached out for a reason. If you won't take the risk, I'll tell you why I think you did."

I felt the anger rise in me as the words seemed to skip my filter running from my lips before I could hold them back, "Why do we have all these people dying of a plague? Why are so many people not wearing masks to protect one another? Why are people who claim to love me supporting a leader who clearly doesn't care about me or other people like me? When will this out of the world insanity end?"

Lorraine saved the day as she place each item in front of Izzie. Izzie leaned back as her basket of fries with a large vanilla malt replete with sprinkles landed right in front of her.

Lorraine said, "Is this all you'll be needing today, Izzie?"

Izzie replied, "I think I'm all set. Thanks Love."

Izzie then raised one side of her lip wryly as if she might laugh, but she grabbed my hands and said, "It's hard to love a world that doesn't love you back. Do you know that much of your younger life, the world loved you when you had very little to offer in return? Have you thought of the hands that held you, the voices that believed in you, or the eyes that greeted you when you had little to offer in return?"

I replied, "So, that's it? So, you give me greeting card answers with a side of guilt? Are you sure you're not related to my mother?"

Izzie replied, "I take that as a compliment. I've never met a terrible mother. I've certainly met broken ones and frightened ones, but I have never met a horrible mother."

I asked, "Can this please not be about her today? She's dead. I'm not. Can we deal with the living today? Just this once."

Izzie reached into her basket of fries and managed to eat five French fries at once dripping in ketchup. She then used her napkin and dabbed her mouth, saying, "Do you want to know about my morning?"

I replied, "Sure. Why not? Tell me more of your half answers with riddles! I can't wait to get lost in more of your profound wisdom."

Izzie grabbed my hands, "Brian, I was at the bed of a woman dying of COVID. Tamara Cleveland is her name. This gorgeous woman became a researcher in ALS after her father succumbed to the disease when she was only twelve years old. I held her hand the last few hours because no family could be with her. They placed her phone next to her ear as her daughter told her she loved her. I held her hands in mine as she took her last breath. Then, Tamara could see me. Tamara then said, 'You're the one that has been holding me the entire time?"

Then, we embraced and wept, two mothers honoring the final footprints of a beautiful soul. As her eyes met mine, she remembered she was more than Tamara Cleveland. Her other names and other shoes and other lives and other children and other stories were all there. Brian, she then smiled and said, 'Well, that was a lesson. That was worth it. It truly was. Thank you kindly, Miss...'

I said, 'My friends call me Izzie.' She embraced me again, and she said, 'Well, I'd better watch out for my two children and my new grandbaby. They will be a mess without me for a while, so I'd better get to their dreams and send as many hummingbirds and butterflies as I can muster."

I asked, "Was she not frightened at all?"

Izzie leaned forward and said more quietly, "Yes, my dear. Everyone agrees to a final breath when they choose their first. There's more to this story, Brian. Can I finish?"

I replied, "Of course. Go ahead with the great story of Tamara."

Izzie smiled and said, "I will, young man. Then, Tamara shocked me when she turned around and looked right at me as if she forgot something. Tamara then said, 'My son! Randall! Is he here? Can I see him?' I replied, 'Yes, Love. He's been waiting.' 'Oh God! I have too. I must touch my son again!'

I said, "Well, did she get to see him?"

"Of course, she did. I placed her hand in his, and they held each other as a force of light rose from them that beamed into the sky. We call that the Embrace. As we reconnect with our beloveds, even the furry ones, a shock of purple light explodes and rises in a plume. We all pause and place our hands on our hearts, because we never forget the Embrace. It is what makes the journey matter. No matter the role we played for those we love, we are always grateful for the moment we can embrace them. She will embrace with five more loved ones. We have learned to let the purple dome of light soften before the next beloved approaches. Each embrace offers the perspective, and the love returns. It is why I love my job."

I asked, "The embrace? Is it organized in advance?"

Izzie then said, "Brian, the embrace is not under our control. Just as you saw Tamara remember and call to her beloved, then they appear. It is a remembering process, and we simply ensure the soul doesn't immediately rush back to their current story."

I said, "How do you ensure every person has someone? Like you, I mean? During times when lots of us die?"

Izzie then reached once again for my hands and held them. Her warmth filled my hands as she said, "Honey, you mean the pandemic. How do we ensure someone like me is holding the hands of every person dying in this very moment?

I said, "Exactly. There are a lot of deaths these days."

Izzie's eyes filled with tears that never quite escaped her eyelids. I had never seen her cry, and this shocked me. We always ensure someone is present. The human world sees this as a train station with attendants for each arriving car, but, for us, we walked you into this life and we are with you throughout the many lessons you have with Death. There are so many moments a soul has with Death. I am there for every one of them. I am your companion that carried you into life and I will be there when it is your time to die. Does this make sense?"

I asked, "A companion? Why are you associated with Death when you are really supporting a Life?"

She laughed heartily at this and drank down a large pull of her vanilla malt. She then said, "Brian, life is a rich passage of memories and lessons that become our stories. Death is why we tell them. How can you separate me from life? Many have tried, and they have never succeed, do they? We know when we choose any beginning that there will always be an ending. Without the ending, there is no story. Can't you see that?"

I asked, "So, why do people choose a life, knowing Death will one day take it all away?"

Izzie leaned back in her booth and crossed her arms. She then looked out the window, and I couldn't help but join her. The small crabapple tree was barren but the blue-breasted finches were eating the dried berries from the branches.

She finally said, "We all have different reasons for that moment. I will choose a life again. I've been in the Department of Death and Dying for many decades now, and I can feel the tug for the chaos and the beauty and the miracles and even the loss. If you watch everyone else dancing on a stage or playing on a field, there is a moment when you must feel the gravity of life once again. I never imagined me wanting to live again after my last life. I'm not ready to tell that story. For that one, I'll need a margarita."

I replied, "I can't imagine choosing this life. I get it. There are moments when everything makes sense and when my feet are perfectly placed on the path. I know those moments but so many others are trying to find the walls to brace me when the fear suffocates me in the dark."

Izzie replied, "Do you remember when you prayed and asked to speak with Death?"

"Yes, I do."

She continued, "I knew you weren't expecting little old me, but this is who you got. I have never told you this part, Brian. You asked me to be your guide in life to better know the mysteries of Death. I'm here because you asked me."

I asked, "When? Why would I even.."

Izzie interrupted, saying, "I was standing with you at the AIDS Quilt in Washington DC as you unfolded those blankets with all those names and faces. I was beside you when you got the call about Marc and Scott and Jimmy and Chuck and... well so many. Too many. You asked me to be the one that would be with you as Death brought the hardest lessons to your feet.

I said, "I have no awareness or memory of this, but I somehow know it's true."

Izzie smiled at me, saying, "Death has taught you more about life than anything else. Do you even see that?"

I replied, "If I'm honest, I don't. Death is cruel. You are a silent ambassador for so much pain and hopelessness. Can't you see that?"

"Love, I can see that from your chair of life, you hold tightly to this body and name and reputation and story. However, you have so many in spirit now. Can you place your hand on your heart and see what life looks like from ther eyes of those no longer living it? Words will fail at describing this perspective, but trust the eyes of those you love to show you a different view."

I asked, "My mother is still my hard one. I can't believe how long she was forced to suffer before you came for her. Why?"

Izzie ate some french fries and took a big gulp of her shake making a loud sipping noise as a ball of cream broke free of the straw, landing in her mouth.

"Brian, I don't have those answers. I know one person who can answer that question far better than me. Have you asked your mother yet?"

I replied, "No. Weirdly, I didn't even think about it."

She continued, "Brian, your beautiful mother looked so at peace as she drifted ever closer to me in those final moments. She looked so frantic as opposed to most souls. She looked at me and pleaded to return, because she was so worried about her boys. You and your brother were the first concerns she carried into my arms as I greeted her eyes.

I told her, "Mary Ann, your father is waiting. He is wise, my dear. He will have some words to soften your worries. Can you trust me?"

She grabbed my hands and pleaded with me, "Can you tell my older son that I'm sorry for the way my life made him feel so alone and full of worry?"

I told your mother, "My dear Mary Ann, worry is a gift. It is a pathway that will lead him to Love. Love holds tightly to people and teaches us to eventually let go."

Your mother then focused on you. She said, "Can you tell my youngest son that I'm sorry for the way I judged him? I thought being gay was wrong. I thought it was all my fault. I felt that I had failed him somehow. Please tell him. I cannot go until you promise me."

I interrupted, "Really? My mom said those words? What did you say, Izzie?"

Izzie replied, "Did you see how her worry and frantic fear was so different from Tamara. Your mother was in a state of complete panic. Then, she finally remembered. The softening of her transition came when I told your mother these exact words,

"Mary Ann, you gave your son a powerful gift. You taught him to accept and love himself. You gave him the perfect gift for his soul. Can you imagine a better one?"

"Izzie, I.... thank you. i never considered this. I am..." I paused, and somehow, the word "mother" being spoken from Izzie's mouth brought her back to life. Her face returned to my eyes, and the soft eyes I had seen in the hardest of times were staring back at me.

I asked, "Is my mother proud of me?"

She replied, "That's not nearly as important as you being proud of her. The ways you imagine she failed you are the ways in which you have failed at love with the world. The way we love our mothers always tells you how you love the world. By the way, that's why you're here."

I then felt my anger rising as I said, "This world has failed me. Why the hell should I need to love a world that has been so cruel and self-centered? We have over a million people in our country that have died, and our infection rates are becoming exponential. This is largely due to jerks not wearing masks and making this about their personal freedom. Is there a way out of this?"

Izzie replied, "There's a way through. Until you see those you judge as your lesson, you will not have peace. Fear is powerful, and belonging is even more so. Belong to them and listen. Listen. Borrow my eyes and see the lesson they are learning and the one you are offered. After all, you've been in the 'pain in the ass role' before. Right? You seriously don't think you can offer the compassion you demanded?"

I replied in my usual way when truth lands at my feet in this way by simply saying, "Yup!"

This is when I know the lesson has finally sunk in. This is when my defeat is my win.

Izzie said, "Brian, Death is the season, and you must choose life. That means all life. Loving this life is about loving the living exactly as they are and exactly as you find them. Did you forget why you chose this life?"

"If I'm honest, I have no idea what I said. How could I?"

Izzie said, "You said to me as I guided you into the womb of your mother, 'I want to learn to love, Izzie. I have had so many lives when those around me loved me in ways I never matched. I want to learn to love.'

"What? It was you? You're my…."

Izzie replied, "You can call me your fairy god mother. That's almost perfect, isn't it?"

I asked, "Izzie, what did you tell me after I told you I want to learn about love. Please tell me everything."

Izzie looked at me and she was disarmed for the first time. Izzie had tears in her eyes, and she said, "Mary Ann, the mother you chose for this lesson in love, will name you Brian. Brian, you literally said to me, 'I don't like that name. Why can't I have a king's name?' I smiled and laughed with you, and then I said, to you, "Brian, you sweet young soul, will learn Love. Your life is a prayer offered and a promise kept. You will learn Love from this mother."

"I did?," I asked.

Izzie asked, "Brian, you have been dearly loved by many in this journey. Wouldn't you agree?"

As I remembered all of the people who had loved me, I could only say the obvious, "Yes."

Izzie grabbed my hands for a final time across the booth and said, "Honey, are you ready to become the love? Are you ready to see every person in your life as a miracle and every painful situation a lesson? It's not the easy path, and you won't become powerful. You'll become softer. You'll become quieter. You won't demand the world hear your story because you will fall in love with their stories."

I could feel the fear rising in me, and I said, "Am I ready to know this Love? I'm afraid I will screw it all up."

I don't know why, but I started to cry. I recognized no tears had been shed since this whole thing began. Not one tear. As I closed my eyes and felt the river of sadness and frustration and anger and heartbreak finally speak, no words could form. Only tears could honor this moment.

"Brian, open your eyes, Love. Open your eyes."

I managed to open my eyes, and I was shocked to see the fifties diner was gone. I was just starting to notice the soft water rushing in a stream sound that I knew well. I looked down and my eyes began to see.

I was in the river. My feet were in the river and the water was moving through my legs as fallen leaves whisked by in the gentle current.

It was the river between this world and the world of light.

I remembered. The sun was shining on my shoulders. As I raised my eyes, I saw her - my mother was there holding hands with Izzie.

My mother smiled and said, "Love this world, my Brian. You are here to know Love in all her dances and seasons. Are you ready?"

"Is it really you, Mom?"

"Yes, my Love. Are you ready to be the Love, Brian?"

I replied, "I don't know, Mom. I'm tired."

My mother stepped closer and I naturally fell into her arms as the river gently moved through us. She whispered into my ear just above the sound of the river, "Brian, love is patient. Love is kind. Love is just. Did you forget those words? This Love starts with how you hold your own story. Tell your story in a way where Love is the beginning, the middle, and the end. When you offer this Love to your story, you will insist every other person know this Love."

"I don't want to leave you again, Mom," I cried.

She rocked me and said, "My Dear One, I never left, and I never will."

My mother stepped back but she held my hands, "I love you. I always will. Now, it's your turn."

Izzie came close to me, and I could see her tears streaming down her face, "Brian, we must say goodbye until another 'Hello!' is upon us. Your mother and I are never far, and I always love a vanilla malt and French fries."

I kept searching for the words of profundity, but instead, I landed on, "Thank you. I now know."

Izzie smiled, and she said, "No, my Love. You remember. There will be a day when I will embrace you, and we will walk together arm in arm up this river on that final day of this journey. You will leave the name Brian and the footprints of this life will become another story of lessons and miracles we will all share. Are you ready to know the other side of Love?"

"Yes, Izzie. I am."

She looked at me and grinned, saying, "You know, that means less whining?"

"Yes, Izzie. I am sometimes just overwhelmed by the empty chairs of life."

Izzie smiled and grabbed my hand in hers. She looked at me with the most serious eyes she had ever offered, saying,

Honey, there are no empty chairs.
Every chair is a story waiting to be heard, held, imbued with life, and celebrated.

That is the greatest gift of all.

One day, you'll see the embrace was always reaching back to you in every empty chair.

The Nuts and Bolts of Mediumship

I was asked by a student, "What are the nuts and bolts of mediumship?"

I thought for a long time, and I said, "Mediumship is about the quality and strength of the link you offer Spirit. Are you able to offer your vulnerable soul to any Spirit hoping to sit with you?"

I came to recognize mediumship requires that we tune ourselves to the vulnerability Spirit requires. So, I've decided to share the very process I use when establishing a link with any Spirit communicator.

1st Step

Ask the question. Every journey starts with an intention. Ask yourself: Am I a medium? I believe we all have mediumistic qualities, but I've come to accept that not every person is called to this as a professional path. However, the journey to pursue mediumship opens other doors for people and provides a level of clarity that will both surprise and inspire people in this river of life.

Place your hand on your heart and ask this question as many times as you need. Close your eyes and imagine a door in front of you. The door says "MEDIUM" on it. Trust the door you see and reach for it. As you approach the door, does it open?

This interaction with Spirit is powerful, and I will never forget doing this activity for myself. I then trusted the answer by checking it five thousand times. I wish I could tell you a more spiritual answer that would make me look cooler, but it wouldn't be true. I held this question for many years until the work clarified the open door. My mind needed to trust where my soul was being guided, and I strongly encourage people to allow the work to assist you in this discernment.

Never give another person doing this work the authority to close that door for you. To me, this is an act of arrogance and a misuse of authority. Teachers are not spirit guides. They are fellow travelers in the river of mediumship learning the lessons their soul is destined to learn through their practice of mediumship. Trust the river and where it will guide you.

Your awareness is so much more important in these waters than another person's experience of this canyon.

2nd Step

Begin to see yourself as a spirit and a person. When you begin to recognize more and more that you are a spirit experiencing a human life, you can invite your spirit to offer a different view of any situation in life. You will come to honor the family to which you belong and understand how the greatest gift any family has offered us is the wound. It is often that wound that led you into this river and into this moment where your unique Spirit, due to all the wisdom and empathy you developed due to the lessons offered in your life, can now be used in service of those in grief. I've come to believe we are all grieving, and the stage of that journey fluctuates and changes for each person or soul we hold dear. Your greatest wounds that have become wisdom will serve you in ways no one can prepare you for. You hardest experiences become chords the Spirit person can use to communicate their messages of healing to their beloveds.

Question: What does my mind think of this situation in my life? What does my Spirit hoping to learn in the lessons of love in this moment? How can I use the forces of gratitude, love, and compassion to expand the very presence of my light in all situations?

3rd Step

How does a medium link with Spirit?

There isn't one right way. I often think of a bicycle wheel as a metaphor here, and I consider every silver spoke as a unique way to find the same sense of connection to the loved ones in the light. As long as your link leads us to an effective connection that serves the evidence and the work, your approach is always up to the medium.

4th Step

Place your hand on your heart.

5th Step

Breathe in and out in five cycles where you inhale for five seconds, hold your breath for five seconds, and exhale for five seconds. There's not a hard and fast rule about this, and there are many breath techniques. However, for me, this is the one that has worked the best.

6th Step

Imagine yourself beside a river. As you are doing your five cycles of breath, lay in the stream of the river with your feet receiving the water traveling in that direction from your feet to your head. The river is warm and immediately comforting. The sandy bottom receives you perfectly, and you notice through the top of the water that the sun is beginning to set. Enjoy your breathing cycles and then relax into a five to six second inhale and exhale cycle without the pause.

7th Step

Say these words:

I offer my feelings to you, Spirit, to use in any way to serve the message
you seek to offer your loved one.

8th Step

I offer my hearing and voice to you, Spirit to serve the messages of love. You are welcome to use my ears or my mouth.

9th Step

I offer my eyes to you, Spirit so I can join your world as a passenger and narrator through your world.

10th Step

Feel the arms of a beloved of yours in Spirit embrace you. Feel their love for you and know they are there to assist you in building your own soul's light. As you maintain your breathing, imagine a ball of golden light is in your third eye. As you exhale, imagine that light growing in all directions. As you exhale, notice the light grows as a bubble that will ultimately contain you. This will likely take three to six exhales. Remember to extend the bubble up and out to the sides.

Your third eye may flutter or feel some pressure. It also may have no physical feelings in any way.

Trust this bubble of light. It is not fragile. It is solid and reliable – rooted deep into the center of the Earth.

Trust your bubble.

11th Step

On the exhale, let go of your presence to the side. Imagine your agendas, needs, attachments, fears, or any other distracting emotion or memory to be placed to the side, ready and prepared to return when your work is done. If you notice any part of your body tightening in the river, focus on that part of your body. That section will naturally soften and allow the gentle warm waters to hold you in the safety of it's purpose.

12th Step

Invite the Spirit to sit with you.

Trust wherever the Spirit guides you and imagine your feelings, your ears, your mouth, and your eyes being offered to them.

13th Step

Trust this new friend and enjoy the miracle of this connection. When the goal of the work is to serve the Spirit, we are no longer attached to the "YES" that forces the work to be about us instead of the healing. The Spirit knows the evidence, the memories, the messages, and the details their loved one requires to trust this connection. When we need the "YES", we will abandon the Spirit and focus on proving we are a medium. Instead, the focus on the Spirit will prove that love is eternal even when our human stories end.

14th Step

This miracle will offer you a peace that will change your life in profound ways.

Invite the Spirit to lead you in your work and trust they know you have the eyes, the ears, the mouth, and the compassion to honor the journey they are offering their loved one.

Trust is a process, not a destination.

15th Step

It starts with trusting yourself.

You are the medium their loved one chose.

You are the light you seek to connect with.

You are the miracle you seek to honor.

You are the grace your soul seeks in the eyes of every person.

Allow that grace to touch your heart too.

Allow that grace to touch your heart too.

Mediumship is not about proving our value; it is about honoring the unseen lines of connection that make all lessons universal and all pain an invitation for connection.

The greatest gift we receive is knowing we are never alone.

LESSONS IN THE PRACTICE OF MEDIUMSHIP

This series of books was designed to address the soul lessons we face through the journey of practicing mediumship and the ethical dilemmas that cross our path in this journey.

However, I heard from many people pursuing the calling of mediumship, and wanted to honor their question. This appendix is designed to very specifically address guidance around the actual practice of mediumship that I hope will be of service to you in your work. Rather than write an essay that captures all of the nuance of mediumship, I have decided instead to share some insights that I hope support you in your journey of the work.

There is no one right way to approach this journey of mediumship and I cannot pretend that I am the authority of this work. I only know that this journey of mediumship has offered me a curriculum in the greatest lesson of life – love. As cheesy as that might sound, I have never been more certain of this.

Lesson 1: Practice, practice, and then practice some more.

I have met many people who become perpetual students of the work. They take classes, work with many teachers, and sometimes participate in circles. There is no replacement for doing the work. The work, more than anything else, teaches you who you are as a medium. In my humble opinion, there is no one else who can do mediumship the way you do the work. I think of mediumship as an instrument of the soul, so I think most of what we are doing to create and maintain a strong and effective link has to do with understanding the spirit body and how the chords of a spirit's story and journey can be played on the notes we offer.

Regardless of how natural our ability is, our work with clients often highlights the values we carry with the work. Clients are the greatest teachers we have, and learning to work with people who carry skepticism, fear, trepidation, and often profound grief, requires experience and reflection to see every obstacle in the work as an opportunity for growth.

Lesson 2: When practicing, consider sitting with clients that are not developing mediums at least half the amount of time you practice.

When we work only with developing mediums, there can be unreasonable expectations the receiving medium places on themselves and unconscious agendas we all carry that create competitive and sometimes unhealthy exchanges. If a medium, having taken a similar amount of courses or a fellow mate that has practiced for a similar amount of time, is sitting across from you for a practice session, it makes it difficult for the mediums in that circumstance to offer constructive feedback due to both the varied styles, beliefs, and personal awareness each person is offering at that time. I've seen too many times where fellow students have been destroyed by someone giving them highly critical feedback often couched by the critic saying they have high expectations.

I had a student tell me all of her reviews about the teachers she had worked with. This student proceeded to be critical of every teacher, and I knew this criticism was going to land on me at some point. It's not personal. When a student has strong opinions about a teacher and their pedagogy, they are doing what many of us have done in other arenas of learning. They are afraid they won't be successful, so some will find someone to blame for their lack of progress. If you are practicing your mediumship with a student in that insecure posture, they will often, without any negative intent, place their critical eye on you.

When someone judges the work of another when they are unable to do that work, it is often motivated by a fear of not believing they can be successful. If you, as the medium, are not careful in protecting your own vulnerability, these exchanges seldom make us more effective.

Instead, we once again place our success in the eyes of another person and their validation can cripple us in our journey. We are connecting to a divine intelligence and a grace that few of us have experienced in this human journey. No matter the outcome, recognizing that this journey is about you and your own connection to the Divine, will save you a great deal of time and headaches.

As you practice with non-mediums, there is a miracle that occurs in this journey. When we launch this journey, we are mainly trying to prove to ourselves that mediumship is real and then we are trying to discern if we can do this work. Because I did not develop in a circle, I am a little biased in this regard. However, as I came to recognize the initial work of trusting Spirit as a friend or acquaintance sat across with me with arms crossed and a deep concern for my mental health, miracles began to occur.

I watched the faces of people as their loved one in spirit enters the space and the journey we take together for that forty-five minutes has become the miracles I depend on whenever I feel like giving up. Collecting these miracle stories when you start and reminding yourself of these experiences when you feel as if you are failing will always carry you through your times of growth. After all, these periods of growth would only occur if we were ready to develop and then offer new chords of ourselves to the work of mediumship. We do call this a practice after all.

Therefore, so many of us feel like we aren't as good as we were a year ago, but the truth is that the miracle that blew us away a year ago is no longer as big of a deal. For me, this is always my inner call to invite even more evidence or surrender into my connections.

We are seeking to deepen with the evidence and offer more and more of ourselves to the Spirit who chose us to work with their grieving family member. We can begin to consider which parts of my instrument am I less willing to offer? Why? As I explore this, I always find new vulnerabilities and connections with loved ones that more deeply enhance the work.

Lesson 3: Mediumship requires you to know you are worth the love you are seeking to honor.

Because we are all helpers, this journey will teach you a lot about boundaries and learning there are times when you need to choose your own well-being. Your grief is just as important as any other person.

Your pain in this life matters.

Your grief journey is a heroic one, and the grace that flows through us in this work must also touch our brokenness. Otherwise, this work can become an endless struggle of not being good enough and never finding peace in your calling to serve both Spirit and the person or families in grief.

If your own grief doesn't get to sing across the notes of your soul, how can you allow the song of love and healing and hope to play across your instrument?

There are times in our journey of offering love and kindness to this world where you will encounter a powerful teacher who will require you to remember that you matter in all of this. They are not my favorite teachers in life. They are often taking advantage of you in some way or seeking to control you to their own demands. We've all been this same teacher for someone else, so there is no comfort of self-righteousness in this acknowledgement.

Mediumship is a journey of seeking the truth and honoring the evidence. There are times when your wounds will become more important than the truth. When you are the consequence of another's lie and judgment, it is a powerful time to remember who you are, or you will allow the world to tell you.

Lesson 4: The fence between what is psychic and what is mediumship is far more complex than many honor.

We are all spirits.

Take that in.

We are all spirits.

As spirits in human bodies, we are opening our hearts to have the light in us connect with the light of those here with us and those in the world of spirit. I began to recognize mediumship is natural and not so different than the way we connect with the spirits of the living. This distinction many demand we make can actually create confusion and turn the practice of mediumship into something stilted, controlled, and make these interactions a staccato style of connection where there is no surrender and the medium is always in charge.

However, when we embrace that we are the Spirit connecting to the Spirit, this connection is natural, vibrant, intense, emotional, and transformational.

Mediumship is made complex by those who need authority in this miracle. If you have a medium that is teaching with these rules and authority, the sacrifice for the developing medium is significant. Many times, we will unconsciously try to earn another's approval in this journey. This will be not so different to a religious organization, because you are once again told this connection can only be accessed by the chosen few.

I am coming to know this communication is our birthright and no one, whether you become a working medium or not, is denied this sacred connection between this human journey and the eternal light of grace that is always reaching to us and anchoring us in ways I don't think we will ever understand until we rejoin our beloveds in the world of light.

Lesson 5: Race matters. Gender identity matters. Sexual orientation matters.

If you, as a medium, do not care about someone's oppression or a person's pain, you cannot tell their story.

It is that simple.

Lesson 6: Your mediumship journey will always be a reflection of your integrity and intention.

No matter how much money one has spent on websites, business cards, promotion, advertising, how many courses you have taken, or what famous mediums you call your teacher, your work will be judged in the world by the quality of mediumship you offer.

We are agreeing to serve people in grief. If we make promises or imagine a level of skill to satisfy our timelines or our demands that we get a return on our investment, the person reaching out to us for a connection to their most important loved ones will lose faith not only in you as a medium but in the very profession itself. That, in no way, implies that we must be perfect and able to please the demands of every client who reaches our way. Rather, it means that our stability and comfort and trust and specificity of evidence will be the benchmarks the world uses to assess your contribution. When you offer someone a powerful connection to their loved one, the referrals will sustain your business far beyond any other means of promotion.

No one can be your evaluator of the moment when you invite the world to see you and receive you as a medium professionally. In the same way that we trust the inner voice of this calling, we must also know that our work is producing consistent results that serve the intent of the evidence and honor the story of the Spirit we are called to serve.

We are also called to serve the grieving heart of people trying to find a way to choose life after a significant loved one has died.

This is a burden and a responsibility few can truly understand outside of this work. We must know that we are in a place of integrity with our readiness. I know this lesson well and I honor I failed at this early on in this journey. I tried to rush this calling into my human timeline and made demands on the world to honor something in me I was not fully prepared to actualize. That risk caused harm to others and I am hoping you will consider a more sincere appraisal of your abilities at this time before you risk the well-being of a person in the chaos and maelstrom of grief.

Your lack of integrity can have a cost far greater than you may see in that moment. That experience of losing faith in mediumship can have the result of a person believing this profession is nothing more than a manipulation and if we make promises we can't keep, they will be right.

When we present ourselves to the world with a demand, they see us in a way that is untrue; it is far harder to have the world believe you in the future.

We will never be perfect in this work, but we must have a consistency to our practice a person in grief can trust and the client will know is informed by the evidence. No one can answer when you are ready. You will never feel perfectly prepared but there will be a confidence and an unshakeable trust in this connection. Regardless of whether you have perfect evidence throughout your reading, you will know you are with a person in the light and you will know they are there to offer a healing far beyond anything your best imagination could conjure. Your doubts will have quieted and your reach to the other side will feel like reaching to a new friend.

Only you will know when it is time and hopefully, you'll have a confidante or mentor that will support you in arriving at the threshold between the world of developing and practicing. The consequences are too great to not demand that the evidence and your integrity be your bellweather in this decision. Mediumship is a lesson in the soul's dance with the Truth, and there is no greater moment than this one to honor the service to the world of light and the world of grief.

Lesson 7: Be wary of the person who presents their beliefs as rules for everyone else to follow.

In mediumship, the journey to the evidence and the connection is like a wheel of a bicycle. There are many pathways to that space where the connection occurs and you, my fellow medium, will hopefully learn to trust the footprints in the snow of your story. They are reminders of the courage required of us every day to trust an unseen love that will carry you into meadows far more beautiful than you ever could imagine. Never allow another person to hold the key to this kingdom. The key never belonged to one person; it was always a universal passage only asking you for your vision, your feelings, your wisdom, and your heart to trust you will know the way.

Others may carry a light for you but you must never forget that you have the light within you to guide your way. The rules others may use to exclude you or to demean you is the prison they inhabit. You decide if you sign the lease for their lesson.

If you give them your power, you too will live behind the bars of their deception and control. This journey will require a lot of dedication, hard work, time, patience and compassion for every person you meet; it will ask you to trust in ways you likely never imagined. The time you dedicate to this journey may not result in you becoming a platform demonstrating medium or even a working medium, but the gift of knowing life wins and love is eternal will feel like payment enough.

This journey will make everything in your life have meaning and every person in your life a teacher of all lessons. You will feel a connection to life that will give you an enduring peace.

When you touch the grace and the love you have always desired, you will have a clarity of purpose and love for others that remind you we are all One.

It is our responsibility to know this gift is enough. The demands we place on this path are about us and the lessons we are here to learn. That doesn't make us more spiritual or less spiritual. Rather, this journey of mediumship is serving the very lessons we are here to learn.

We are the light of stars and constellations guiding travelers across oceans to new lands. I'm coming to realize the grace flowing through us in this miracle is a constant orbit in our hemisphere – reliable as the moon's dance across our evening skies.

Her dress unfolds against the galaxies in an astrolabe the greatest discoverers used to chart this world. Whoever invented the astrolabe somehow knew the world's wonders and miracles would only be discovered if they trusted the light of the night sky. It is a dance holding hope in one hand and an insatiable curiosity in the other. It is the deepest call of the heart – intimacy and connection.

So, mediumship is a mirror of the very wounds and internal rapids we face every moment of every day to love the world. We observe, but we are always in the river. We imagine ourselves to be on the shore, safe and protected. However, we are reaching out to anchor one another in the shared journey of grief and hoping to find meaning in the chaos of the rapids of loss.

What are we to learn? To swim? To surrender? To pray?

Before my friend Jane died from liver cancer, she said, "Look for me in the moon. If you look closely, you will see me, smiling and dancing. My death is a moment, but my love is forever. Maybe, I can remind you that your death is a chapter, but our lives are the story."

The chair of mediumship that awaits you will tune the chords of your own experiences and invite you to choose life in new ways.

In the journey of collecting miracles, one day, you will know you are also a miracle.

You are an instrument of this symphony and a narrator of the human story.

What is asked of you in return is everything, even your shame, your regret, your heartaches, your lies, your joy, your miracles, your passions, your dreams, your trauma, your experiences, and most of all, your vulnerability. These chords of your experience will be tuned against the touch and connections with every soul who chooses you to build a bridge of hope for every client you serve.

What you receive, in return, is nothing less than life itself.

Epilogue

EVERYTHING I LEARNED ABOUT MEDIUMSHIP, I LEARNED FROM A DRAG QUEEN

At first glance, you might be thinking this is a ridiculous comparison that is only being utilized to sensationalize this work and even could potentially dishonor the sacredness of this calling.

However, for me, drag queens have throughout my life shown me, through their courage and convictions, how to love the world that may never love you back. They embody the energy of their drag persona, blend with the authenticity of this persona, and honor the complexity of identity that exists within all of us.

At the age of sixteen, while attending a Catholic all-boys high school, the drag queen culture is the family that received me. Their memories and stories appearing on these pages honors the courage and grace these souls extended to my broken one at a time when my very life was on the line.

There is no greater act of courage in life than choosing to be who you are, accepting many will not be able to ever honor or understand that choice.

So, click your heels and remember home is in the eyes of every person who sees the truth of you and celebrates it.

Lesson 1 - Coming-out as a medium is not an event; it is an on-going process that requires great courage and vulnerability.

I will never forget when I came out as a gay man by finally getting the courage to go to the under 21 bar called Stars where there was always a drag show before the dance floor became electric. Being so young in the bar scene made me incredibly vulnerable and placed me in situations that were sometimes very dangerous, including everything from drugs to sex. I was a sophomore at an all-boys Catholic school, where obedience and conformity were valued above all others.

Balancing that world with the early gay bar scene took some negotiating and a lot of compartmentalizing. The more comfortable I became with being who I was, the more risk I would accept in "coming out" to the world around me.

I came to recognize that the more I accepted the man staring back at me in the mirror everyday with bad acne, bad hair, and questionable fashion sense, the better my life became. I started to feel the word 'gay' differently over time, and I became prouder and prouder, accepting and honoring the women and men who came before me that allowed my access to the gay community to even be possible.

After my friend Kim received one of my very first readings as a medium, she said, "Brian, have you decided if you're going to tell your parents?"

I paused and replied, "Well, honestly, how much worse can it be for them? I feel so badly for my dad. I get to tell him his out and proud gay son now thinks he can chat with dead people! How much more can my poor Catholic father take? I should just tell him I'm Satan's mistress first."

Kim looked at me with her earnest eyes and didn't laugh one bit. She replied, "Honey, God is using you to serve people in profound grief. Don't you dare demean this calling or yourself. If you need everyone to accept you or understand this, you won't ever find peace in this work. You cannot love people through this work if you need them to validate you all the time. Do you know what I mean?"

I said my deeply measured and spiritually evolved phrase that always seems to serve every occasion by saying, "Yup."

As mediums, our journey to accepting ourselves and coming-out about who we are will be as unique as we all are. There isn't one way to define this process, but as a famous drag queen once said, "When you become the image of your own imagination, it's the most powerful thing you could ever do." (RuPaul Charles, 2017)

What the world thinks about us is none of our business; but what we believe about ourselves influences the success of every single action we do in life in every arena. So, this might be a great time to chat with the voices in your head and get them on your team STAT! The world can only hurt you if you agree with the judgment they throw your way.

Lesson 2 – Embody another person's essence.

"Hell! I don't know! Belinda Carlisle? Madonna?," I said, knowing Miss X was not at all interested in my assessment of which famous eighties music icon I should become to attend the following week's ball.

Miss M looked me up and down: jeans and a shirt depicting Bart Simpson holding a skateboard with the words "EAT MY SHORTS!" written across the bottom. She was not amused. My drag family, although it wasn't as formal as that, had decided I needed to join the crew at the following week's ball and at least try to not be so pathetic and dreadful. I agreed to comply and Miss X said she would accept the duty to transform me into "anything other than this mess." She had her work cut out for her.

I arrived at 6:00 P.M. for the two-hour marathon of makeup and mousse, designed to show me the route to becoming the best drag queen in Denver! After Miss X and our mutual friends Brandon and Ricky got involved too, it was starting to come along. Miss X chose Belinda Carlisle and I was to lip-synch to the song "Vacation" by the Go-Go's, one of my all-time favorite groups.

Miss X announced, "Here she is! Grab this goddess a mirror and me a martini!"

As I stood in the mirror, Brandon grabbed me some heels to wear. I stepped into the heels and he said, "Now, walk like a queen."

I had a blonde curly wig and blue eye shadow. I had a black jacket with shoulder pads and a white skirt. I looked like a Chucky doll that survived a plane crash filled with flesh-eating zombies. That's being kind.

As I tried to strut my stuff, my ankles kept giving out and I looked at all of them. I said, "I can't do this. I am not..."

Miss X looked at me, and she said, "Honey, when I first put on a dress, I felt free. I want you to feel that rise up in you as you walk the runway, because every path is a runway now." She snapped in a half moon arc almost in perfect sequence. I looked in that mirror and tried to let the energy wash over me.

Brandon said, "Let the essence of Madonna rise up in you. Think of what a badass she is and how she..."

Miss X interrupted, "Bitch, this is not Madonna. Does she look like Madge? I think not. This is that Belinda bitch from the Go-Go's."

Brandon replied, "Oh! I see it! I have an idea." He removed the curly-haired wig and wrapped a white towel around my head and added some pink lipstick. I looked like one of the girls from the Beauty and the Beat album. I was getting excited.

Miss X said, "Wait! Before we go out and make fools of ourselves, let me ask you one question, Brian? How do you really feel wearing drag?"

I looked at myself, and I replied, "Like a fraud. I can't do this. It dishonors what you do. It feels tacky and I am not shaving my legs!"

With that, my drag career ended, but I saw how seriously my friends took the process of unfoldment to becoming the spirit and presence of whoever they were imitating or becoming. It wasn't as slapstick and over the top as I'd always imagined it to be.

I saw Brandon transform into Miss Krystal. I will never forget how different they both were. He became her. They were, for all intents and purposes, two different parts of his soul stepping forward. I felt relaxed and playful with Brandon, but Miss Krystal scared me. I never knew what comment would fly out of her mouth, but I always looked up to her for her courage and presence. It wasn't a game for her; it was an expression of another part of her. This display of courage overwhelmed me at that time, but I always knew it was a confidence I would need to discover within myself in a different way.

Lesson 3 – When you honor what makes you unique, you come to recognize these are the chords of your soul Spirit plays to honor their ties and lessons of life.

"I only do this once a year now," Miss Velvet said as she prepared to go onstage at the Max Bar in Omaha, Nebraska.

Vince, a tall handsome man with short silver hair, tucked-in shirt with Levi's 501s with button-up fly and a love of cologne, transformed into a drag queen that left me breathless. He became a new person. This gentle soul transformed into Miss Velvet, a tall southern woman with long black hair.

As Miss Velvet approached the stage, she was carrying a mattress on her back lip-synching to "I Will Survive" by the real and oh so powerful Gloria Gaynor. She rocked that glittery purple dress and, in heels, Miss Velvet collected tips as the Posturepedic mattress went side to side with every thrust of her hips. People cheered and screamed as the song ended.

After Miss Velvet greeted her adoring fans, I approached the reigning queen, saying, "Are you sure you should only do this once a year?"

She walked over and held me close, squeezing me to her foam core chest, saying, "Look Baby, I am more certain that one night a year is all my ankles can take. Miss Velvet takes a lot more energy than I can muster. Besides, the more I am Miss Velvet, the less I feel like Vince. Do you know what I mean?"

"No", I replied. "Isn't it like Halloween? You dress up once a year for fun, right?"

"I'm not sure if this will make sense, but I am Vince to the world, but part of me is Miss Velvet. She's not an act; she's an expression of who I also am. Does that make any sense?"

I replied, "If I'm honest, I don't understand. Are you saying that you're a woman trapped in a man's body?"

Vince looked down, and I could see how frustrated he was with me. I wasn't seeing him, so, once again, he had to explain the beauty of him because I didn't have the mind or the heart to see all of my dear friend. The box of his gender was all I was able to see in that moment.

"Brian, it's not like that. I'm Miss Velvet and I'm Vince. They aren't separate people; they are different expressions of me. Does this feel like an act?"

It never had. In fact, I looked forward to this night because I had grown to love Miss Velvet.

"So, Vince, I…"

"Brian, I'm Miss Velvet tonight. Can you prove to me that you see me?"

I said, "Sorry, Miss Velvet. It makes me sad you can't be you more nights. Do you know what I mean?"

Miss Velvet smiled from ear to ear in a way I had never seen. She then leaned forward, and said, "Well honey, you just might get a kiss tonight. The truth is that I have evenings at home when I put on the wig and Miss Velvet returns. She is an aspect of me that needs to shine."

As mediums, we are in the unique position to honor all aspects of a person. We use the authenticity of us, the desire to connect, and our own wounds to resonate with the loved ones in the light. The greater we honor our own wounds, the more we can resonate rather than react with another.

Lesson 4: Drag queens teach us that we cannot truly serve others if we need their approval.

In the journey, the work of mediumship can feel like seeking the next 'Yes', but this places an undue burden on our clients. At some point, we seek the validation from within. We come to know that resonance and trust it, even when the client isn't saying 'Yes'.

My first teacher in this level of inner stability was when I met Nicole Nikki. When I was sixteen and trying to discern what it meant to be gay, this group of drag queens adopted me when they met me at a local club aptly called 'Stars'. Using a fake ID, I would go into this club underneath the viaducts in the city of Denver, which was surrounded by the railyards and a distinct smell of dog food in the air because of the local Purina plant. In other words, it wasn't a fancy setting to discover who I was, but it was an experience of community that saved me.

Nicole Nikki was the first person in that bar to greet me. She took me under her wing, and she said early on, 'We can never put this muffin in a dress. He's got three left feet but he hugs like a teddy bear. He can be our brother but let's be clear. I am his drag mother, and he is part of us." As a young gay kid attending high school at an all-boys religious school, having someone claim me when all of my identity was in the room is an indescribable blessing.

Before we would head to Stars on a Saturday night, we'd all get together and hang out as the queens got ready. That was a process that took longer than any marathon. They also found a fake ID that allowed me to hit the twenty-one and older clubs, so I was included in my culture for the first time. As we all sat around waiting for Nichole Nikki to exit the bathroom, she called all of us to the door as she said through the door, "I am ready to show you who I really am. I've been scared to let all of you know, but it is time. Are you ready for me to emerge the butterfly I've longed to be?"

We all screamed with glee and encouraged her to let us know who she really was. We all looked up to her and found a sense of family many of us had never known.

Then, she emerged from the bathroom with a bathrobe. She immediately threw open her robe, and announced, "I'm a woman, Baby! Now, I've got the parts to prove it!"

As she stood there, we all were in awe of this transformation, and in front us, stood a beautiful woman. Her face softened with tears as we observed her taking her first new steps as the person she'd always known in her heart. Now, the mirror honored what she knew all along.

Whenever I struggle to say the words, 'I am a medium' for fear of being judged or misunderstood, I always remember the mother who chose me when I wouldn't choose myself. I think of the courage when she opened her robe for her naked body to be celebrated, witnessed, and blessed in a world of snap judgments.

She was beautiful and powerful as she allowed her body to be seen, because her body finally aligned with the soul she brought to this planet.

I remember her.

Nichole Nikki died of AIDS as did so many other lovely souls that taught me how to be part of a chosen family.

I remember her.

As you more and more see, feel, and honor the medium inside you, there will be a moment when you know you are perfectly imperfect for the adventures that lie ahead. When it is time to share your calling with your friends, your family, and the worlds you inhabit, never forget the courage of others who risked far more than us to claim who they are in a world unprepared to celebrate the beauty and the miracle of that moment.

Imagine Nichole Nikki and the faces of any soul in Spirit cheering you on. Remember that every action you take to step out in faith, you give everyone you love permission to do the same.

The wake of love she and many others created for me in life remind me to take the risk to be seen and to see because I've been given the privilege of growing old, a condition denied to most of the people who embraced me in my 'coming-out' journey.

Is there a better way to honor our loved ones in the light than to trust the calling of the heart?

Lesson 5: Be fierce with the truth and gentle with every student.

Pinky Pie is one of the best drag performers in the world. She is taller than six feet with the vocabulary of a drunken sailor and the soul of a wise guru. When my friend Jared steps into the shoes of this alter personality, he becomes Pinky. It is a stunning transformation and the courage she embodies as Pinky invites everyone in her presence to feel the love and strength she carries to any person lucky enough to see her in action.

"Tonight, we're here for a reason, Bitches!," Pinky screamed. "The mother of a third grader who completed suicide is with all of us tonight. This beautiful boy was being bullied for being gay, and the stress and pressure this created in his world was simply too much. How many of us can relate?"

I looked around and watched as almost every hand was raised. I looked to the right and saw I had raised my own. It was a strange feeling to have in a gay bar on a Sunday afternoon. As our hands all honored that we had all been in the river of suicide, Pinky walked over to the mother she invited to honor her son's life and ensure the lessons his life offered all of us spoke to each and every heart and soul in that room. Bullying kills, and a child's vulnerability to honor their sexual orientation and gender identity deserves a respect and grace, because when a child is lacking that support, their very life is on the line.

Pinky said, "Hey Queens! We've got a Mama Bear who needs our love tonight. The cruelty of this world took her son from us, but we will come together tonight to ensure this courageous mother knows she is not alone in this world." She looked directly at the mother, handed her flowers, and the money that was raised at this event.

Pinky then said, "We would all be lucky to have had a mother with the love and compassion you offered your son. It proves that the world must also do our part to love every single child of God. We've got so much work to do on that front, but we must never lose faith. Can I get an Amen?"

We all cheered and then, the music started. Pinky was lip-synching to Adele's "Fire to the Rain" and she ended her routine with hula hoops and high kicks that any Rockette would have celebrated. As Pinky finished her routine, the house gave her a standing ovation worthy of the queen mother she truly is.

Pinky took a profoundly painful event in this mother's life and created an event that truly celebrated her son and took all of us to school in the process. As Pinky emanated her strength and power, we all walked away feeling her strength and knowing we could persevere through any challenge the world placed at our feet.

As I walked to my car, Pinky had transformed into Jared. He still had his makeup on, and I was afraid of how to address him. Then, he said, "Did you have a good time?"

I replied, "Are you Pinky now or Jared?"

He replied, "I guess I'm both if I'm honest. In this moment, I'm not on a stage and not doing anything inappropriate with a hula-hoop. So, I'm Jared."

I fanned out like a crazy fan in desperate need of a bouncer, saying, "You are so freaking amazing!!! The way you reached out this mom in grief is a great example. I'm so glad she came."

"Brian, that was me. That little boy who ended his life in a closet was me. I considered suicide every day and I still can't believe I made it. The second we tell the truth about our own story, any person who knows the pain and anguish of suicide will know you are a person safe to tell your story. Isn't that amazing? Simply by being real and authentic, we invite everyone else around us to be who they are. I only have five minutes to love the crap out of every person in that bar, so I must open my heart and not let my fear get in the way of the tornado of love I hope to hit every single heart. You never know if that hug will be the one that gives someone else the hope required to choose life another day."

For me, this could not be a better summary of the purpose of mediumship or the reason to continue to grow in this vulnerable dance against the fear that we are not enough. When we are willing to take a risk every day in our work to continue to open our heart to the loved ones in the light, we will likely never know the hope offered to the person in grief. The love that goes through us and not from us will always land on the hearts that desperately need it. We only need to have the courage to open our heart, even when our fears tell us we aren't good enough or worthy of this calling.

We open our hearts anyway.

Printed in Great Britain
by Amazon

18591262R00161